THE ULTIMATE REIKI SYMBOLS GUIDE

EXPLORE 65 UNIQUE SYMBOLS

MASTER THE LANGUAGE OF SPIRITUAL HEALING FOR
HEALTH ∞ ABUNDANCE ∞ SPIRITUAL GROWTH

VLAD DIMANCEA

ReikiScoop

2023

Co-founded by Vlad Dimancea and Petre Veluda, the ReikiScoop brand is part of Vell Consult Intermed SRL.

First published as a digital e-book in 2023.

First print edition in 2023.

Printed in various locations by print-on-demand services.

Published in Romania.

Author: Vlad Dimancea

Cover design: Petre Veluda

ISBN: 9798862855319

Medical Disclaimer

The information contained in "The Ultimate Reiki Symbols Guide" is intended for informational and educational purposes only. At ReikiScoop, we consider Reiki a complementary way of healing that is intended to support well-being efforts, not as an alternative therapy that replaces traditional medical treatment. While the practices and theories described herein are believed by some to promote general wellness, they are not intended to replace or substitute professional medical advice, diagnosis, or treatment.

Neither the authors nor the publisher of this book are licensed medical professionals, and nothing in this book should be construed as prescribing, diagnosing, treating, or preventing any disease or medical condition. If you have any health concerns or are taking any medications, you should consult with a healthcare professional before engaging in any practices described in this book.

The authors, co-founders, and publisher expressly disclaim any liability, loss, or risk, personal or otherwise, that is incurred as a consequence, directly or indirectly, of the use and application of any of the contents of this book. Readers are encouraged to consult with healthcare providers and follow their advice and judgment concerning individual health matters. Your use of the information in this book is at your own risk, and neither the authors, co-founders, nor the publisher will be liable for any damages arising from your reliance on it.

A MANUAL FOR REIKI ENTHUSIASTS

Table of Contents

Bring The Essence Of Reiki Symbols To Life

Imagine holding a key - not just any key, but a key to the universe. Now, imagine that this key isn't a tangible object but a symbol, a pictorial essence that embodies profound spiritual power. This power can unlock doorways to diverse energies, information, and entities, bridging the physical and spiritual worlds.

Welcome to the fascinating realm of Reiki symbols, a unique cornerstone of the healing arts that has resonated across cultures, religions, and ideologies worldwide. These intricate representations are far more than just art. When used with respect and understanding, they are keys that can offer insights into the most profound aspects of existence.

Immersing yourself in the realm of Reiki symbols is akin to learning a new language, a language that converses with the universe. As you delve deeper into their meanings and functions, you'll start to perceive symbols not as static images but as dynamic conduits of universal energies.

However, it's essential to approach this journey with an open mind, free of prejudices. Our tendency to label things as positive, negative, or neutral may create a superficial understanding, limiting our full comprehension of these powerful spiritual tools. Let's unravel this tendency and expand our understanding, recognizing that each symbol is a unique manifestation of energy and information.

The Nature Of Symbols

The term 'symbol' can be traced back to the Greek word 'sumbolon,' which means 'token.' Later, it became part of Latin as 'symbolum,' which we still use today in many languages.

Symbols depict manifestations, expressions, or phenomena with valuable information and an energy signature. In the spiritual world, they become keys, unlocking doors to varied energies, information, and entities, creating a bridge between the physical and spiritual worlds.

> *" Symbols bridge the physical and spiritual worlds. "*

Now, it's natural to categorize symbols as positive, negative, or neutral. But here's a crucial point to be made: symbols aren't inherently good or evil. They have unique vibrations and represent different physical, energetic, and spiritual concepts. Some symbols connect us to positive energies, while others tap into lower vibrations. Even so, any symbol can be used differently by changing its structure.

The true power of a symbol lies in how we choose to wield it.

Example: Beneficial Symbols Used For Evil

Consider the swastika. In Hinduism and Buddhism, it's a spiritual symbol signifying aspects of life and death. In Sanskrit, it means "helpful for your well-being." Its history dates back thousands of years, originating from another high-vibrational symbol - Antahkarana.

The Antahkarana can be used for multiple healing purposes and helps connect one's subconscious (inner self) with one's conscious part (mental self) harmoniously.

However, during World War II, it was repurposed to manipulate the masses. The result? The symbol that once stood for well-being became a symbol of terror. This shows how a symbol's energy can change based on how it's used.

The red, black, and white colors and their excessive presence created the ideal design for infiltrating one's subconscious. From there, any message associated with this symbol became second nature to most people. Many became subdued without knowing how to protect themselves, and their free will was crushed.

In essence, people have the ability to attribute and/or change the energy level of a particular symbol for a specific purpose.

4 Guidelines For Using Symbols

Remember that you have the power to modify a symbol's structure and, with a specific intention, can give it an entirely different role. However, like everything in life, any action has its consequences.

Some spiritual practitioners base their entire knowledge and evolution on symbols, while others don't pay much attention to them. I believe symbols are quite useful and can add a lot of value. Yet, it's crucial to acknowledge that true evolution comes from the work you do within yourself.

1. Every symbol has a distinct purpose linked to universal energy. And, no symbol is "better" than another;

2. Most symbols have hidden properties yet to be discovered through meditation and similar techniques;

3. Understanding a symbol's form, significance, and energy functions is crucial for a healthy connection. But remember, being proficient in energy work doesn't necessarily mean knowing all symbols. The highest level of spiritual practice is when you don't need tokens or talismans;

4. Always get consent before using symbols on others to avoid practicing 'energetic aggression,' which can have serious karmic consequences. I'm sure we've all had times when we wanted total control over a situation. Still, true wisdom comes from letting go and merging with the universal energy;

" Being at peace is far superior to being correct. "

Categories Of Symbols

The Graphic Representation

Symbols can serve as potent vehicles for communication, much like written language. Take, for instance, the ancient scripts of civilizations like the Egyptians, Mayans, or those from Easter Island. These cultures didn't rely exclusively on spoken or written words; they harnessed the power of graphical symbols to convey intricate concepts and deliver comprehensive messages.

These symbols, often referred to as hieroglyphs, continue to intrigue us today, with some remaining undeciphered, hiding their secrets from the modern world.

The Artistic Representation

Artistic representations of symbols are another fascinating category where a single image or a sequence of symbols encapsulates a broad concept or profound notion. This use of symbols is notably prevalent in Asian cultures, particularly in China and Japan. The origin of their letters and writing, known as Kanji, traces back over 3000 years.

With this unique symbolic expression, the Chinese and Japanese could condense complex phrases or sentiments into a single, harmonious sign. This elegant art form continues to be valued today, with Kanji scrolls remaining highly coveted items.

The Practical Use

Symbols also find practical applications in various rituals, meditations, and practices such as Reiki, Qi-Gong, and Alchemy. Here, symbols serve not just as artistic expressions or representations of spiritual ideologies but as functional tools that aid in therapy, guide practitioners through pivotal life moments, and cleanse the mental and emotional bodies.

To fully harness their spiritual and energetic potentials, practitioners often undergo attunements or initiations to align themselves with the unique frequencies and energies of the respective symbols.

In essence, symbols carry profound weight and influence in our world, ranging from complex historical languages and artistic expressions to practical spiritual and therapeutic tools. Their diverse uses and potentials continue to captivate, inspire, and assist humanity on our collective journey of understanding and growth.

NOTE: *This handbook begins by presenting the fundamental knowledge of Reiki symbols. Following that, there is a list of lesser-known symbols not part of the traditional Reiki system. You can access the latter through meditation, drawing, or chanting. You can also print them out and place them where you feel will bring the most benefits. Each symbol is defined through its known properties and my experience with each.*

How Reiki Symbols Function

Reiki stands out as one of the most influential spiritual practices, capable of harmonizing the emotional, energetic, and spiritual bodies while promoting healing. It serves as a gradual but reliable catalyst for spiritual growth, enhancing one's understanding of the inner self, higher self, and the world.

Within the Reiki systems, each symbol holds a distinct purpose. As mentioned earlier, no symbol is considered superior to another. Each establishes a connection with various vibrations, energies, and entities. While all Reiki symbols are deemed beneficial, their true impact lies in the way practitioners choose to apply them.

Reiki Symbols General Uses

- Cleansing and balancing energetic structures;
- Aligning and opening the chakras for better energy flow;
- Clearing mental and emotional blockages;
- Expanding your mental field to acquire new perspectives on the physical and spiritual realms;

- Enabling energy transmission across distance and time through dimensional openings;
- Establishing connections with different entities, such as angels or archangels;
- Facilitating grounding and abundance on all levels;
- Assisting in connecting to the healing energies of both Earth and celestial realms;

Remember that whenever you use a Reiki symbol, you are accessing a manifestation of the universal life force energy. Each of these manifestations can be guided toward your inner healing and spiritual development.

You are a channel through which the universal life force energy flows.

Then, with the help of the Reiki spirit guides, angels, or archangels that each symbol connects to, you can manifest those elements into the physical world.

I was once asked:

'Why do we need so many levels and Reiki systems if we have access to such a strong flow of universal energy through the Reiki attunement?'

'Because each level and Reiki system can access a certain part of the universal life force energy.

This segment is directly correlated with your level of understanding, vibration, and evolution at that point in your life.

We live in the physical plane.

Therefore, we are subject to the physical laws.

We need a gradual, step-by-step development, or else the amount of power would be too great and might create mental and emotional havoc. Everything must be done in harmony.'

That's why considering a gap between attunements can help you better assimilate and comprehend the energy and information received.

How To Activate The Reiki Symbols

There are 3 elements you need to consider when activating a symbol to help manifest its unique role and set of properties into the physical realm.

Set A Clear Intention

Intention resembles the foundation for a house. At this stage, you must know why you're activating the symbol and the specific outcome you're after. Even for a basic self-treatment, having a clear goal before you start is key.

Draw The Symbol

Some symbols are easier to remember than others. However, knowing its general shape, what it does, and when to use it matters. So, avoid getting stuck in every line.

Use your index finger to trace the symbol, or concentrate your energy with a "mudra" by bringing your thumb, index, and middle fingers together.

Another way is to use your entire hand. This is a representation of all the elements that need to manifest into reality coming together.

As you grow in understanding, you'll find that the symbol's energy integrates with your energetic fields, deepening your understanding and simplifying its use.

Say The Symbol's Name

When you pronounce the symbol's name three times while activating it, its energy and properties will enter the physical world. Furthermore, this procedure allows you to integrate its power into your life.

Again, don't worry too much about mispronouncing the name or forgetting a line or two. These don't have to be perfect.

Your intention sets the tone so the activation process flows smoothly.

Mastering Symbol Integration

Your vibration rises with each attunement, opening up new realms of spiritual growth and access to a variety of spiritual tokens.

While it's often common practice to receive an attunement to fully unlock a symbol's potential, this guide shares a different perspective.

Believe it or not, some symbols don't require attunements.

When deeply connected to the universal life force energy, you can resonate with and harness the power of any spiritual token.

Allow me to explain - If you have the Usui Reiki level 2 attunement, you're already connected to a higher manifestation of universal energy that provides you with the opportunity to connect with symbols. This connection makes integrating these tokens far easier than before the attunement. Furthermore, this integration isn't limited to symbols from official Reiki levels.

Here's the key insight: Constant practice is the real key to integrating a symbol - whether it belongs to a Reiki level or not - within your energetic body.

In a nutshell, attunement to a symbol can mean one of two things:

- You've gained access to that symbol, but you still need to actively work with it to fully integrate its essence;
- You've used the symbol so frequently that it becomes part of your energy structure - like an extension of your spiritual body;

But… what if you want to work with a symbol you don't have an attunement for?

There are 3 ways to do it. They might take a bit longer than a regular Reiki attunement, but with patience, dedication, and discipline, you'll start to tap into its power.

#1 Meditate On It

Remember that symbols have unique vibration levels and connect to specific manifestations of the universal life force energy. You can visualize any of the symbols in this guide using simple, self-guided meditations. This way, you may connect to their energy print and gradually incorporate them into your structures and daily life. But know that a proper vibration level is needed to receive all the symbols' benefits.

Here's how you can meditate using a simple meditation with the intention of integrating a symbol's energy print and the information it offers through the web of universal life force energy. This should take about 10-15 minutes:

PREPARATION

- Find a quiet moment, away from distractions;
- In order to feel more comfortable and become in tune with your inner self, play some relaxing, high-vibrational music;
- You can also light some incense sticks, frankincense, Palo Santo, or whichever type of incense resonates with you. Also, you can accompany this by lighting a candle, minding flammable materials;
- Sit in a chair with your back straight and place your palms in Gassho (prayer position);
- Close your eyes and slowly take 10 deep breaths to empty your mind from stray thoughts;
- Place your palms on your lap facing upward, close your eyes, and relax;
- Call upon your Reiki guides to assist and support you in this meditation for optimum results;

MEDITATION

- Visualize the symbol you want to connect to right in front of you - notice its size and color;
- Mentally activate Cho Ku Rei + Sei He Ki + Hon Sha Ze Sho Nen between you and the symbol with the intention of connecting to its energy print and information;
- Watch as the symbol starts to glow and as its energy flows toward your energy fields;
- At one point, you become engulfed in the symbol's energy and vibration, allowing it to infuse your body;
- As you slowly become engulfed in the symbol's vibration, you are gradually assimilating its energy and information;
- Remain like this for a couple of minutes and notice the physical and energetic changes within your body;
- When you feel ready, gently open your eyes;
- Repeat this practice daily or until you feel you've fully integrated the symbol's energy and information according to your current needs and vibration level;
- This process will enhance the process of "tuning in" to the energy print of that symbol;

#2 Activate It

This method goes hand in hand with the first one. After you've completed the meditation, try to use it directly.

Activate the symbol in your palms and rest your hands above your chakras, or use it in the Reiki self-treatment. Generally speaking, the more you activate and learn about a symbol, the more you connect and integrate it into your energetic structure. Don't worry excessively about replicating its exact shape because it's your intention and relationship with that symbol that matter most in the activation process.

#3 Display It

At first glance, this may seem simplistic, but seeing a symbol stimulates your brain to connect with its vibration. Having a symbol in sight provides a steady stream of energy that can prove beneficial over time. Activate the symbol using the method outlined earlier in this guide. Do it daily for a continuous flow of energy. These methods might take a bit more time, but with each step takes you closer to mastery.

" The journey of a thousand miles begins with one step. "

- Lao Tzu

Usui Reiki Symbols

Usui Reiki Ryoho, developed by Mikao Usui, serves as the introductory system for many practitioners. It comes with fundamental yet potent techniques that lay the groundwork for all other Reiki systems.

Reiki generally translates to "universal energy," with Rei denoting 'universal,' and Ki symbolizing 'energy.' Thus, the primary objective of any Reiki system is to enable practitioners to channel this universal life force energy. This conduit relies heavily on the specific system's capacity to attain a certain vibrational level within the universal life force energy's nexus.

There are three principal levels in Usui Reiki, to which one can be attuned. While some Reiki teachers split the third level into two sub-categories, 3a and 3b, others consider 3b an entirely separate stage, similar to a 'level 4.' However, this division is justified because The energy and knowledge each attunement provides are quite meaningful, making it imperative to reserve time between them to fully absorb and understand the received wisdom.

Reiki Level 1 - The first level has a more earthbound approach, focusing on teaching practitioners to detoxify their physical and emotional bodies through daily self-treatments. There are no symbols at this level.

From Reiki Level 2 And Beyond - You begin to tap into the complete energetic and spiritual potential of Reiki symbols.

" Symbols are the jewels of Reiki but not the practice itself. "

Working with them will offer many insights, reveal new opportunities, and help you experience the vast nature of the universal life force energy. You'll use them to enrich your experience and better focus the universal life force energy toward a specific outcome. Still, the tangible results we seek will come from the intention and awareness we develop along the way.

CHO KU REI

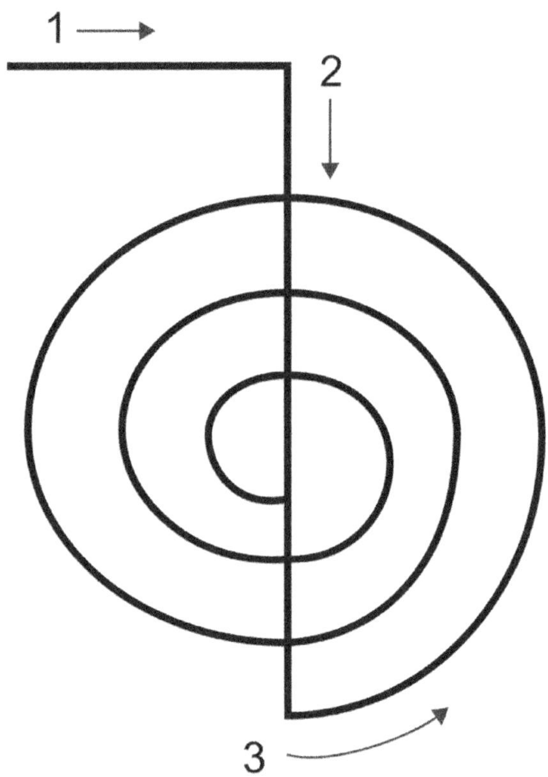

Cho Ku Rei is the first symbol you learn at Usui Reiki level 2. It's probably the most versatile of all Reiki symbols when it comes to its uses.

Cho Ku Rei has three main attributes:

- It helps remove negative energy from a chakra, an organism, a space, or an object;
- It activates and opens an energetic structure to the life force energy, therefore allowing it to heal over time;
- It also protects that structure, person, or object from unwanted exterior influences;

Cho Ku Rei has the following uses:

- Acts as a "light switch," meaning that it offers that spark of universal energy needed to start a Reiki self-treatment or treatment on others;
- Amplifies the energy of any other Reiki symbol when used together in a sequence;
- Drawing it on your chakras will cleanse, activate, and protect them at a significant level;
- When used in self-treatment, it removes blockages and allows the vital energy to flow more freely throughout your body;

- Place it on the walls, ceiling, floor, corners, and middle of the room to disperse residual energies and low-vibrational entities;
- Activate it on food and drinks to cleanse them of residual energies and provide a boost of positive energy;
- Visualizing or drawing it between you and another person or an angry animal can create a barrier of energy that wards off malevolent intentions.;
- Cleanse your crystals or other objects by activating Cho Ku Rei on them. This will also add a small field of protection;
- If activated around your body, it will cleanse the trans-personal chakras that are located outside the physical structure. Also, it will have an overall cleansing effect on your aura;
- Through the Reiki treatment, Cho Ku Rei can help lower anxiety levels. For a more thorough calming effect, apply the symbol on your third eye chakra, including the back projection;

Cho Ku Rei represents one of the many spiritual keys to unlocking a higher consciousness. Therefore, meditating with this symbol can unravel new ways of healing.

Cho Ku Rei Variations

3D Cho Ku Rei

When visualized or drawn as a coil around the body, it is exceptionally good at protecting you from negative energies. It does so by creating a robust, energetic field around you. Start from the top of the head down, and slowly visualize/draw the coil descending to your feet.

Reversed Cho Ku Rei

A reversed Cho Ku Rei will pull out energy from a person, living organism, or object. It is very useful when applied to a hyper-energized person because of its calming effect. A reversed Cho Ku Rei should always be used for therapeutic purposes and with the other person's consent.

NOTE: *Some practitioners might have initially learned Cho Ku Rei in its reversed form. However, the clear intention behind its application is what truly matters. Always remember that this symbol acts as a spiritual token and isn't limited to a single direction of use.*

SEI HE KI

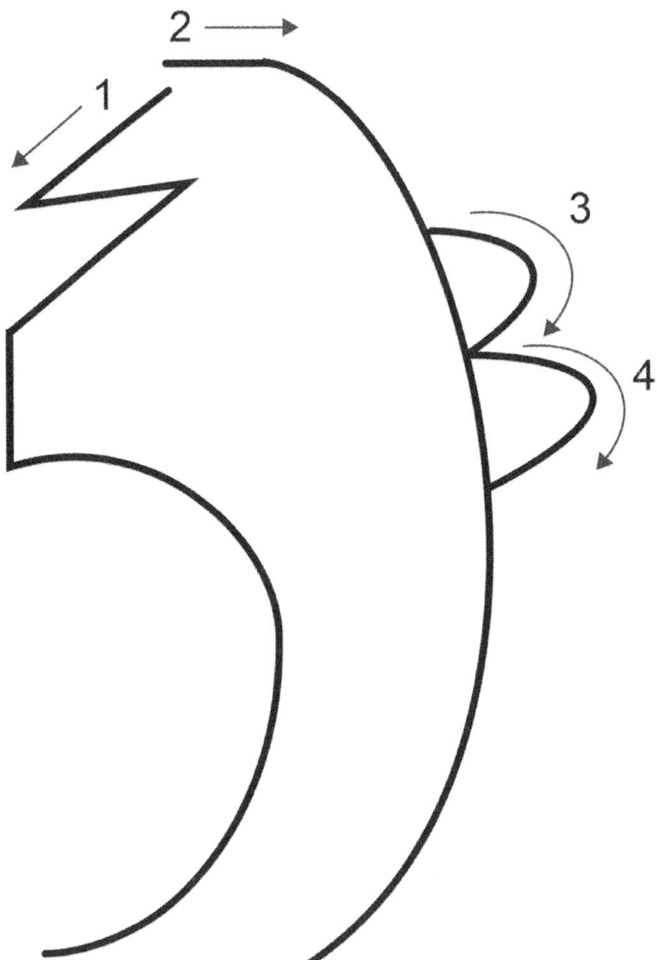

Sei He Ki is the second symbol you learn in the Usui Reiki system, known for its mental-emotional properties.

Sei He Ki has 3 main attributes:

- It helps open an energetic structure, allowing it to release its residual energies;
- Brings harmony wherever it is activated;
- Balances and cleanses the mental-emotional structure;

Sei He Ki has the following uses:

- Using Sei He Ki in your Reiki self-treatment considerably enhances the flow of universal life force energy through your body;
- Activate it on your palms and chakras to enhance the health of your energetic fields;
- Constantly using it in self-treatment will help heal the mental and emotional layers. This means that the energy behind this symbol will help you bring the root of any mental or emotional imbalance to the surface. From that point on, you can better understand yourself and start healing low-vibrational energies such as anxiety, fear, or depression;

- Using a double Sei He Ki above the head (one on each side of the brain) will balance its energetic structure, creating an aura of light and harmony;

- Sei He Ki acts as a small gateway opener. Therefore, whenever you want to have a better connection with your higher self and with the universal life force energy, use it above your head (on the Soul Star chakra). This will help open the channel toward receiving divine wisdom and information;

- For deeper cleansing and activation, you can apply Sei He Ki together with Cho Ku Rei on each primary or secondary chakra. This will bring a higher flow of energy alongside harmony on all levels;

- Activate Sei He Ki during a conflict. You will notice how everyone will gradually back down at one point. Their level of aggressiveness will diminish, and the possibility of ending the conflict peacefully will increase;

- Sei He Ki can help release the negative energy of a painful area and help restore it. After cleansing the low-vibrational energy, apply Cho Ku Rei to enhance the healing effect. This happens because the two symbols are a perfect combination for regenerating damaged physical and energetic structures;

- Activate it on the walls, ceiling, floor, corners, and the middle of the room to energetically cleanse the space and bring harmony;

- Placing a single Sei He Ki between you and another person creates an almost instant emotional and energetic transfer. This transfer will align with your current resonance. On the other hand, using Cho Ku Rei + Sei He Ki will create a harmonious interaction between both of you;

An essential use of Sei He Ki is its ability to help remove addictions and negative mental patterns. By adding the correct intention within the daily Reiki self-treatment, you can use Sei He Ki to gradually remove any addiction and replace negative affirmations with positive ones.

Sei He Ki serves as a beacon for mental and emotional balance. Its multifaceted applications vary from healing inner turmoil to fostering harmonious interactions, consolidating its reputation as a conduit for inner harmony and higher self-connection.

TIP: *When you practice the Reiki self-treatment, try to focus the energy of this symbol on the third eye chakra and sacral area. This will ease the overall process of mental and emotional healing.*

HON SHA ZE SHO NEN

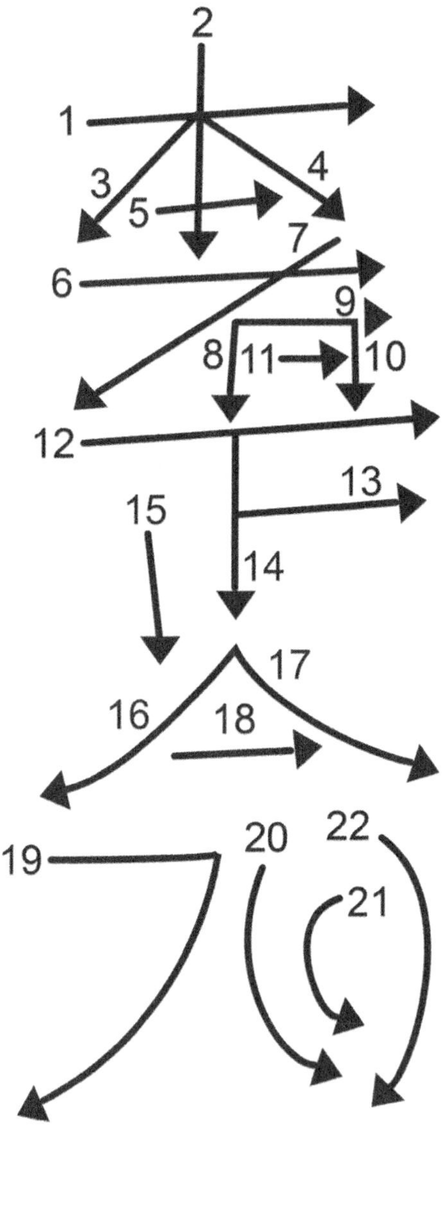

Hon Sha Ze Sho Nen is known as the Reiki distance symbol. Its complex structure enables practitioners to surpass time and space when using the universal life force energy.

Specifically, this is the spiritual key that when used alongside the other symbols, enables you to send healing energy toward the past, present, and future.

That's why Hon Sha Ze Sho Nen is quite a "game-changer" in the Reiki practice. The symbol itself has a higher vibration, uniting the basic Reiki practice with a more nuanced approach.

Hon Sha Ze Sho Nen has 3 main attributes:

- On its own, Hon Sha Ze Sho Nen opens a connecting gateway toward an event or person but without the energy transfer;
- When used alongside the rest of the Reiki symbols, it allows the transfer of energy anywhere in time and to anyone, regardless of their location;
- It possesses keys that unlock gateways to various manifestations of the universal life force energy;

Hon Sha Ze Sho Nen has the following uses:

Use the Cho Ku Rei + Sei He Ki + Hon Sha Ze Sho Nen sequence to transfer energy in the past, present, future, or across distance. You may also apply it backward for the same effect.

- This combination can open a dimensional gateway together with an energy transfer that can reach any situation or anyone at any time, regardless of their physical location;

- Healing your past means helping yourself solve certain karmic debts. Remember to use this method only once or twice a week for about 10 minutes per session. Traumas need time to heal. Therefore, too much universal energy can be detrimental to the number of negative emotions generated from past traumas. You want to avoid bringing them back;

- Create a Reiki project focused on both material and spiritual gifts. When doing so, remember to add *'for my greater good'* to ensure the optimum result for you, which might differ from your expectations;

- Use Cho Ku Rei + Sei He Ki + Hon Sha Ze Sho Nen to send energy to your future plans. This energy will clear the path toward your optimum result and make things a lot easier to handle when those events unfold;

- You can improve your relationships with partners, family, and friends by sending energy to the present and future using the same sequence as presented above. Just remember to add *'for the greater good of everyone involved'* and send energy to the concept of relationship rather than to each person individually;

- Use the same sequence on the crown chakra to strengthen the connection to the universal source of life force energy. Activate it in the middle of the room, with the intention of opening the gateway toward the universal energy and filling the space with pure light;

- Through a self-guided meditation and by using the presented sequence of symbols, you may connect and channel information from higher spiritual dimensions, including the Akashik Records. As a result, you will receive the amount and quality of information suitable for your current level of vibration and understanding;

- Meditation on this symbol can reveal new ways to harness various energies for healing and spiritual growth;

- Activate this symbol together with Cho Ku Rei and Sei He Ki on each chakra for deeper cleansing and activation. When doing so, try to notice the difference in energy flow during the Reiki self-treatment;

- Use Hon Sha Ze Sho Nen in meditation to connect to a place that fills you with joy and serenity. This can be a real place or somewhere in a higher dimension. Call upon your Reiki spirit guides for support;

SHIKA SO

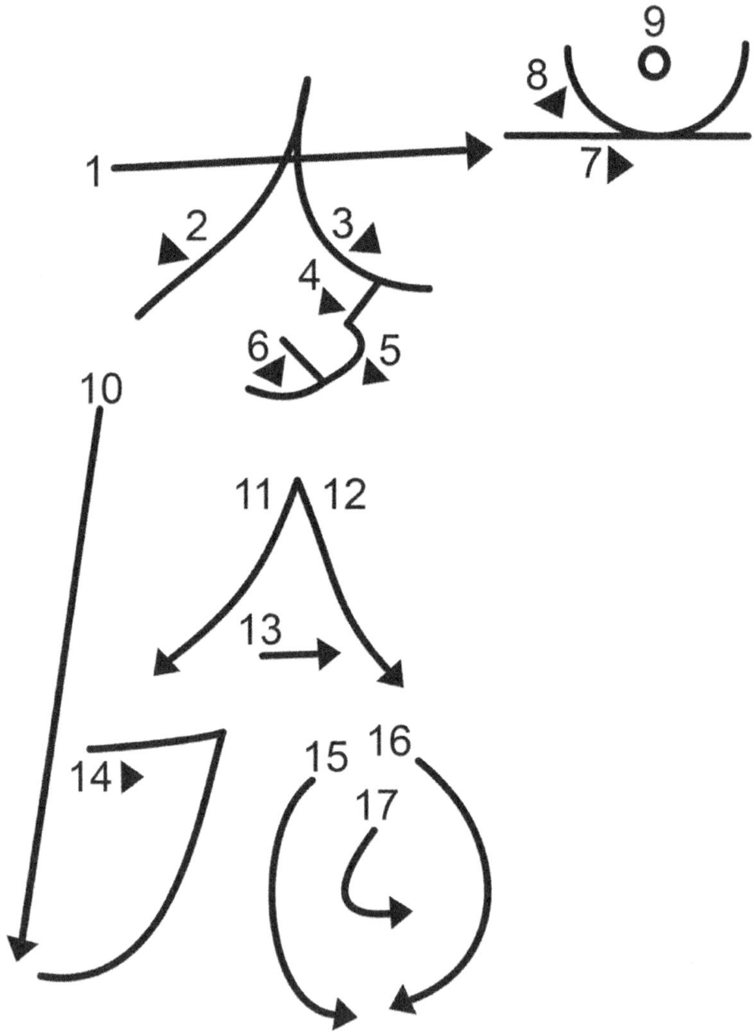

Shika So, while not part of the traditional Usui Reiki system, is an influential symbol dedicated to enhancing communication and healing throat-centric issues.

It aids in resolving physical ailments like laryngitis and thyroid imbalances and fosters emotional expression and clarity in interpersonal exchanges. Therefore, Shika So is mainly used for healing the throat area and stimulating the throat chakra.

Shika So has 3 main attributes:

- Helps heal physical issues at the throat level;
- Opens up your communication abilities;
- Stimulates the harmonious expression of your emotions;

Shika So has the following uses:

- Within the Reiki self-treatment, Shika So will gradually help you express your feelings and emotions, helping you unclog this area. It works wonders with Cho Ku Rei and Sei He Ki, as these two symbols help amplify the effect;
- When used in self-treatment regularly, Shika So helps with a variety of health issues like cervical spondylosis, pharyngitis, laryngitis, hypo, and hyperthyroidism;

- Consider Shika So in therapy to help remove stage fright and gain more confidence in social circumstances;

- Together with Cho Ku Rei and Sei He Ki, it helps combat feelings of seclusion and shyness while fostering self-confidence;

- Activate Shika So on the throat chakra to gradually cleanse and open it while enlarging its energetic field;

- When activated within the center of a room, Shika So will enhance the need for balanced expression and communication;

- Activate Shika So between yourself and another individual to enhance communication. Be aware that it can surface the truth, which is not always what people want to hear;

- Use it during a meeting to encourage discussion and understanding between the people involved;

- Visualize Shika So + Sei He Ki + Serpent of Fire on your lower back to ease the connection with your inner self. Use your spiritual guides to assist you in this process;

- You may also consider using Shika So to improve your connection with your guardian angel and your spirit guides. Cho Ku Rei + Sei He Ki + Hon Sha Ze Sho Nen + Shika So will help filter out their message and eventually understand what they are trying to tell you;

SHIKA SEI KI

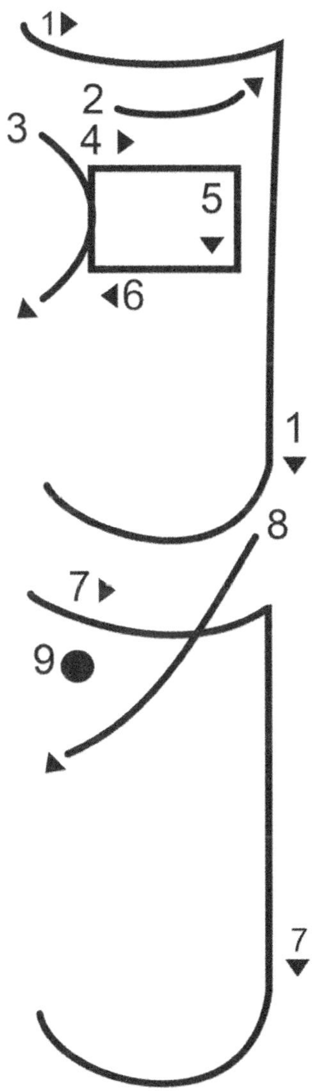

Shika Sei Ki, the second non-traditional symbol from the Usui Reiki system, primarily focuses on the heart, addressing both its physical and emotional imbalances. Beyond mending wounds, it purifies the soul, ignites the heart's energy center, and transforms grief into joy. This unique Reiki symbol is a powerful agent for peace, helping to release pent-up emotions, boost confidence, enhance communication, and heal various heart-related ailments.

Shika Sei Ki has 3 main attributes:

- It cleanses the structure of your soul and activates the heart chakra;
- Helps heal most heart-related diseases;
- Helps heal emotionally related imbalances;

Shika Sei Ki has the following uses:

- Shika Sei Ki can be activated on the palms, crown, and heart chakra. Do this before the Reiki self-treatment to enhance the flow of energy and bring a feeling of compassion toward yourself and others;
- When activated on the heart chakra regularly, Shika Sei Ki can transform depression or grief into compassion and joy;

- It's also known as a symbol of peace and harmony. When drawn into the center of a room, it will promote a loving and peaceful environment;

- This symbol can concentrate a significant amount of universal life force energy at a single point;

- Use Cho Ku Rei + Sei He Ki + Shika Sei Ki to cleanse your soul from residual and negative energies while gradually restoring the lost parts;

- Activate the Shika Sei Ki + Cho Ku Rei sequence on the thymus gland (the 'youth gland') to stimulate its activity. This will help grow your confidence levels and bring a feeling of joy and optimism;

- Use Shika So on the throat chakra and Shika Sei Ki on the heart chakra to stimulate harmonious communication and let go of unexpressed feelings, frustrations, and stagnant emotions;

- Because this symbol aids in directly expressing inner emotions, it can also address and prevent other physical imbalances in this area. These can vary from tachycardia, arterial hypo, hypertension, ischemic heart disease, asthma, and even prevent Angina Pectoris. Whenever you feel sad, melancholic, or even depressed, use this symbol on your heart chakra;

- Shika Sei Ki can help you regain your emotional health gradually from past traumatic events, break-ups, or painful losses;

DAI KO MYO

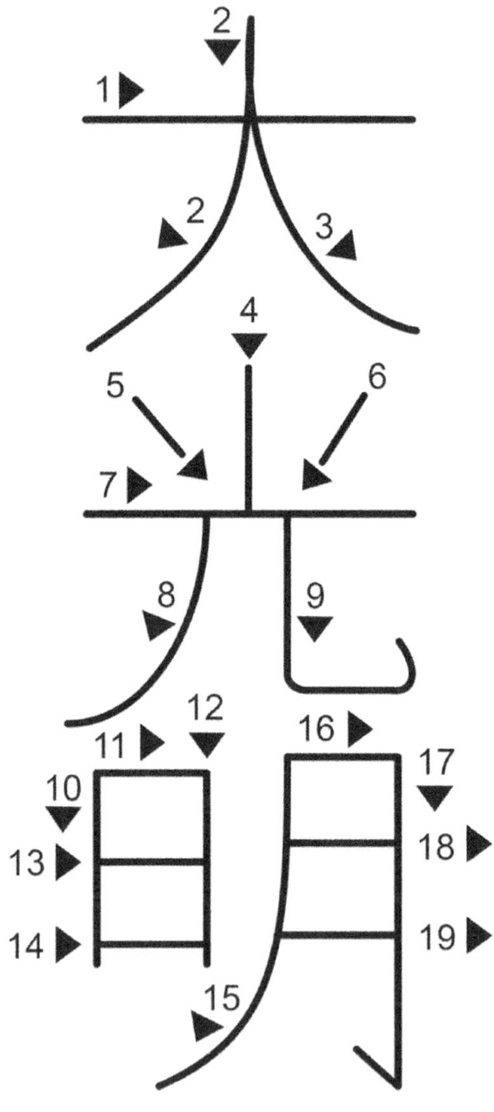

Dai Ko Myo is the master symbol that is received at Usui Reiki level 3. It represents the "Great Shining Light," and represents one of the highest attainments in the practice. Dai Ko Myo facilitates the creation of a strong bond to universal energy, purifying the surroundings of negativity and enveloping situations with pure energy.

Dai Ko Myo has 3 main attributes:

- Creates a direct connection to the universal life force energy;
- It can envelop individuals, objects, or situations in a web of pure energy;
- Eliminates negative energies and influences wherever applied;

Dai Ko Myo has the following uses:

- Activate it on your palms and chakras alongside the other Reiki symbols before self-treatment. Try to notice the difference in the flow of energy;
- Apply the Sei He Ki + Shika Sei Ki + Dai Ko Myo sequence on the heart area to cleanse and recover the lost parts of your soul;
- It plays a crucial role in the "meditation in motion technique." This is something you learn at level 3, and it's designed to help you cleanse the energetic fields;

- Activate Cho Ku Rei + Sei He Ki + Hon Sha Ze Sho Nen + Dai Ko Myo on the crown chakra to intensify the flow of universal life force energy through the entire body;

- The same sequence of symbols can be used to send distance healing (transcending time and space). This can be directed toward a person, situation, or event. Dai Ko Myo will enhance the effect by offering an abundant flow of universal life force energy;

- You can use it to cleanse a room from residual energies. Draw it in the center of the room either by itself or in combination with the other Reiki symbols;

- Deeply cleanses crystals from residual energies and negative projections;

- Visualize Dai Ko Myo inside your brain to eliminate negative thoughts and energies and promote clear thinking and awareness;

- Meditating on this symbol helps establish a deeper connection to the universal life force energy, tapping into its myriad benefits;

- If you intend to activate the symbol on behalf of someone else, position it above their crown chakra. This will help them regain access to the universal life force energy and enjoy the benefits that come with it;

TIBETAN DAI KO MYO

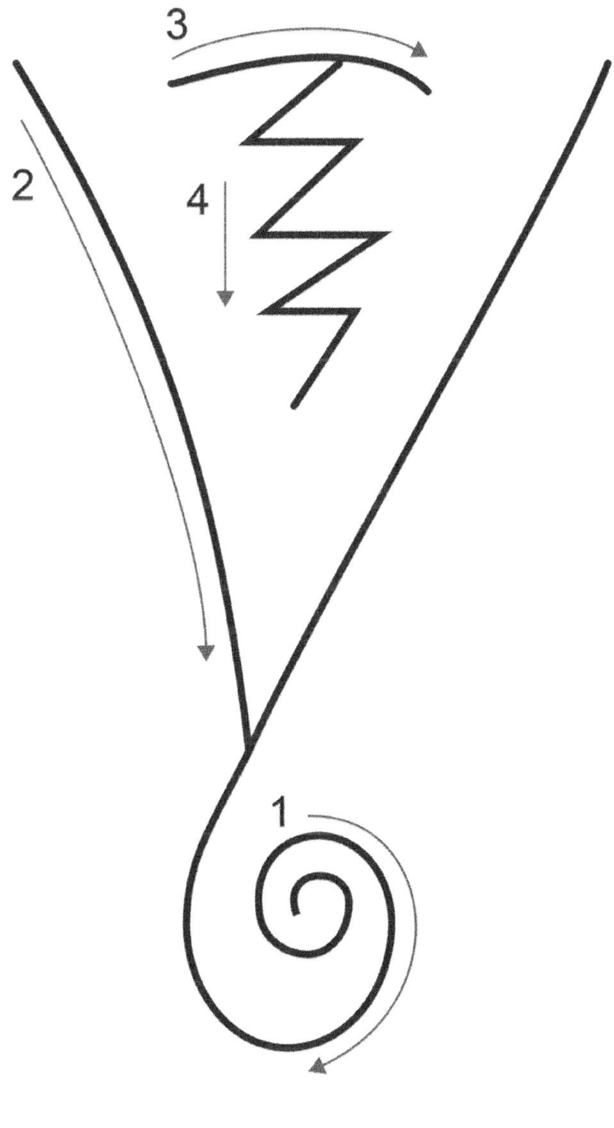

Tibetan Dai Ko Myo is used in the attunement process of many Reiki systems. You gain access to it at Usui level 3b (or level 4 in some schools). That's why it's also considered a master symbol. It holds an ancient power within it, and some practitioners believe that its vibration is even higher than Dai Ko Myo.

Tibetan Dai Ko Myo has 3 main attributes:

- Facilitates the dragon/violet breath during attunement. This allows the student to receive the Reiki symbols and the flow of the universal life-force energy;
- Removes energetic blockages when used in therapy;
- Deeply cleanses a room from negative energies;

Tibetan Dai Ko Myo has the following uses:

- In the master/teacher attunement, you draw it with the tip of your tongue behind the upper incisors before releasing the dragon/violet breath to facilitate the opening of the crown chakra and the main energetic channel of the student you are about to attune;
- Draw it above your head to remove negative projections. Add Cho Ku Rei to enhance the flow of energy;

- Place it in the middle of the room alongside the regular Dai Ko Myo. This intensifies their effect and speeds up the cleansing process;

- Helps cleanse the sacral area, where the Kundalini energy resides. One can use Cho Ku Rei + Sei He Ki + Tibetan Dai Ko Myo on the sacral area (lower back) before the Reiki self-treatment. Notice the difference in your connection with the Kundalini energy;

- Balance your chakras by activating the symbol on their back projections;

- Using Tibetan Dai Ko Myo in self-treatment can help remove many energetic blockages and facilitate optimal energy flow;

SERPENT OF FIRE (Nin Giz Zida)

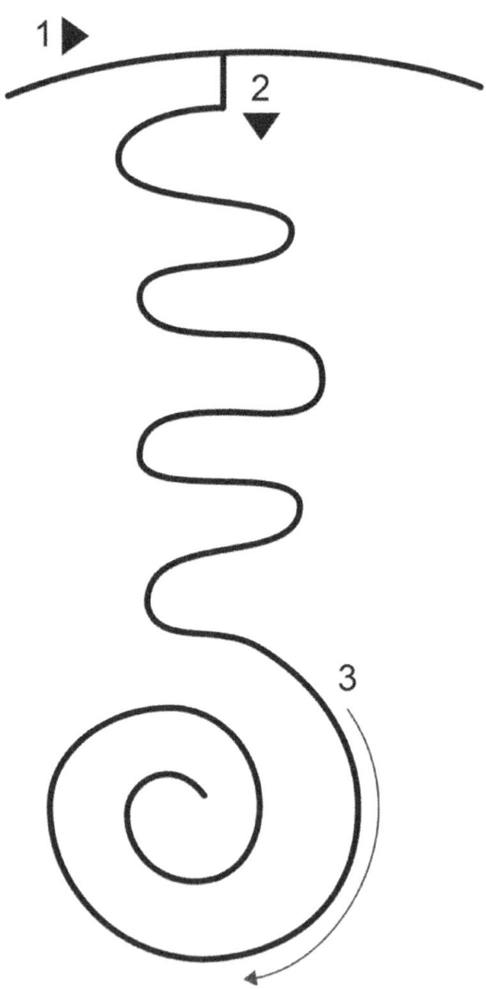

Although not a traditional symbol, the Serpent of Fire is used predominantly at the beginning of attunements and in deep, inner self-healing sessions. It's present in various Reiki systems, including the Usui Reiki Master level.

Serpent of Fire has 3 main attributes:

- It is drawn at the beginning of attunements to align the chakras and center the student's Kundalini energy;
- Clears the energy through the main energy channel;
- Grounds the student, creating a balance between the universal life force energy and the telluric energy;

NOTE: When activated on a person's back, the arch spans from the left to the right shoulder. The seven small arches symbolize the cleansed energy flowing through the chakras, culminating in a spiral at the sacral area.

The Serpent of Fire has the following uses:

- In combination with Cho Ku Rei and Sei He Ki, it helps clear your main energetic channel, Sushumna;
- When you activate CHO KU REI + SEI HE KI + Serpent of Fire parallel to the ground, it opens up the energetic pathway to wherever you need to travel, clearing out any energetic blockages;

- When activated on the back, it flushes away residual energies, increases the vital energy flow, and grounds you;
- Activate it on your body's front side to induce a state of inner peace;
- Use it in conjunction with other Reiki symbols at the center of a room to promote a stable and harmonious environment;
- Use the Serpent of Fire before self-treatment or treatment of others. Activate it in your palms to enhance the energy flow. This will allow for deeper healing of the inner self;

DRAGON OF FIRE

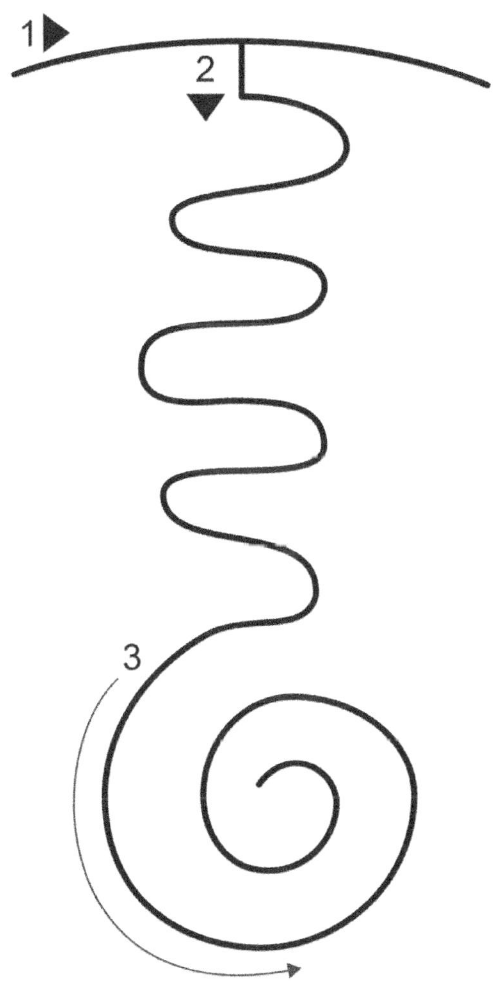

Similar to the Serpent of Fire, the Dragon of Fire is present in many Reiki systems, including Usui's master/teacher level. However, it's not a traditional symbol.

The Dragon of Fire has 3 main attributes:

- It establishes a healthy connection to the Earth's energy;
- Can help you become a balanced channel between the universal life force energy and the telluric energy;
- It can also help treat female genital-related ailments;

NOTE: *Similar to the Serpent of Fire's structure, you can draw or visualize it on the back and front of yourself and others.*

The Dragon of Fire has the following uses:

- Draw it on the body's posterior (back) to gradually relieve menstrual pain and related symptoms;
- Activate it with the Serpent of Fire on the body's posterior to help align the chakras and boost vital energy. Ideal in challenging physical situations;
- Use it for grounding on the body's anterior & posterior;
- When used in conjunction with Ho Ka O Ili Ili or Cho Ku Rei, it can repel malevolent projections. However, the sender may become aware of this effect;

RAKU

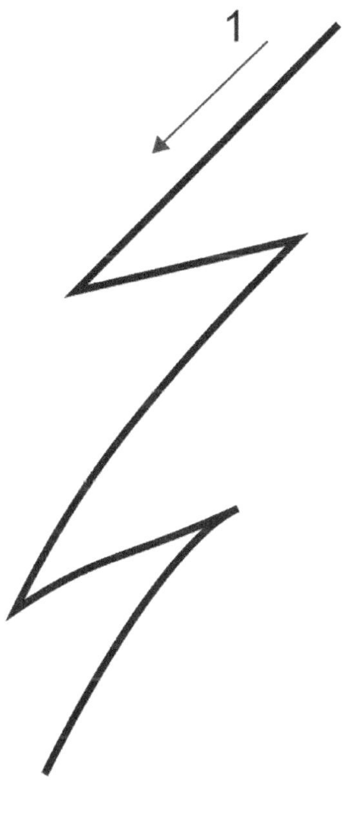

Raku is the final symbol you learn in the Usui Reiki system, present at the master/teacher level. It's debatable whether this symbol belongs to the traditional system.

Raku has 3 main attributes:

- Helps separate the student's and teacher's auras;
- Repels unhealthy patterns and promotes healing;
- Offers a strong grounding effect;

Raku has the following uses:

- Activate it on the body's posterior (back) to help flush residual energies, offering grounding and stability;
- After an attunement, the master/teacher has the right to apply this directly on the student's posterior (back) or between them to separate the auras;
- When used in self-treatment or therapy on others, you can guide its energy to help prevent addictions;
- Cut the energetic cords of a toxic relationship;
- When activated on your palms before the self-treatment or therapy on others, Raku acts as a "lightning bolt" of energy. This clears the aura and chakras of residual and negative energies. For an enhanced effect, add Cho Ku Rei + Sei He Ki;

Karuna Reiki® Symbols

Reiki Master and Teacher William Lee Rand introduced the Karuna Reiki® system to the world. In comparison to Usui Reiki, this system resonates at a higher vibration. This elevated state is possible because Karuna Reiki® helps establish a connection with the energies of archangels and ascended masters. Through its specific meditations, one can initiate the healing of their inner self and gradually forge a connection with their higher self.

Karuna Reiki® or Usui

Think of Usui Reiki as a tool for enhancing physical and emotional health while subtly raising your overall vibration.

Karuna Reiki®, on the other hand, aids in breaking down mental and energetic obstacles through heightened awareness, paving the way for your spiritual growth. In essence, Karuna Reiki® represents the "next level" in spiritual understanding and evolution.

However, it's crucial to recognize that...

One system is not inherently better than the other. Each serves unique purposes and is suitable for different stages of a practitioner's journey.

Karuna wouldn't exist without Usui. Like all things, Reiki evolves, and we have the privilege to discover new applications.

Each level of Karuna Reiki® stands for a spiritual threshold and provides new symbols that connect to higher vibrational energies. Moreover, these tokens reach the energy print of specific archangels and/or divine entities. Thus, you go beyond the standard practices of Reiki and toward the realm of divine intervention.

While exploring new forms and systems of Reiki can be transformative, it's equally important to honor and appreciate the foundations from which we begin. Find peace within yourself and seek value in what you already have. Embark on this step only when you're genuinely ready and not lured by false promises. Understand that this moment might never arrive, and that's perfectly okay. Find peace within yourself and seek value in what you already have.

ZONAR

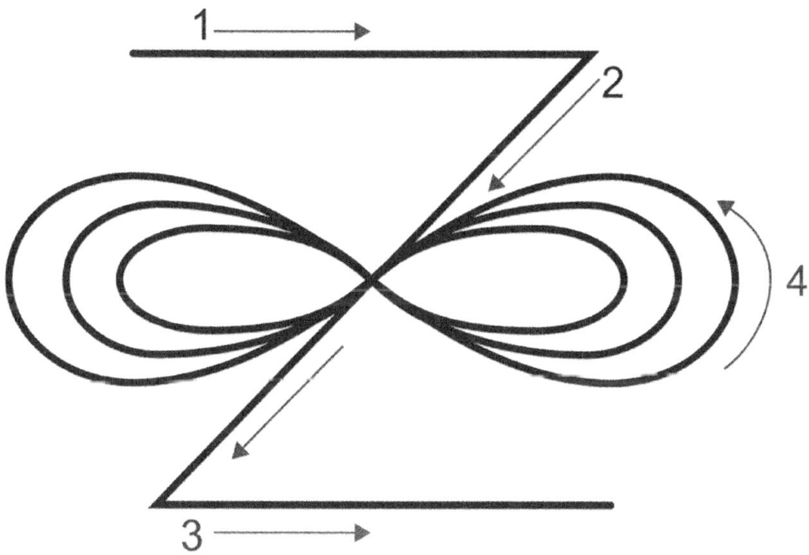

Zonar is the first symbol you learn in the Karuna Reiki® level 1 and was channeled by Marcy Miller.

Zonar has 3 main attributes:

- Helps heal past and present emotional traumas and/or imbalances;
- Offers energetic protection, especially when combined with other Reiki symbols;
- Connects to Archangel Gabriel;

Zonar has the following uses:

- It can be activated on your palms and chakras alongside the rest of the Usui Reiki symbols, offering an enhanced energy flow;
- It is believed that we store most of our emotional and spiritual experiences within the DNA sequence. Therefore, we can use Zonar to access the energetic print at a cellular level and offer deep, complete healing;
- When used in conjunction with Cho Ku Rei, Sei He Ki, and Hon Sha Ze Sho Nen, Zonar helps heal most of the past emotional traumas or imbalances within the self-treatment;

- When sending energy into the future using the same sequence of symbols, adding Zonar can assist in addressing and preventing future emotional issues;

- When placed on a wound or damaged body part, Zonar gradually helps heal the energy structure of that area by rebuilding its energetic field. Add Cho Ku Rei to enhance the effect;

- Zonar acts as a direct link to Archangel Gabriel's energetic print. Therefore, the symbol will help you connect to him through an inter-dimensional gateway. From there on, we can ask for his help or support whenever needed;

- Zonar also acts as an emotional "remedy" for relationships. Whether you use this symbol in self-treatment or treatment of others, applying Zonar will bring gradual mental and emotional stability for the people involved;

- In meditation, Zonar can help us disintegrate unnecessary and/or harmful patterns that keep us from reaching our goals. Visualize it within you and allow it to slowly change your body's vibration;

- Zonar aids in healing emotions such as grief, sadness, pain, excessive jealousy, anger, and frustration. A healthy introspection, together with the Karuna Reiki® self-treatment, helps you gradually remove these destructive elements from your life;

- When directly sending energy toward your past with the intention of healing certain events or situations, add Zonar next to your regular Reiki symbols. Just remember to do this process no more than twice a week for about 10 minutes per session;

The ability of Zonar to access emotional imprints at a cellular level highlights its unique potential. Think of Zonar as a master key that unlocks the deepest chambers of our emotional and spiritual self. It doesn't merely skim the surface but dives deep, targeting the roots of emotional traumas. Diving deeper into the realm of Zonar, its association with Archangel Gabriel signifies its profound connection with messages, clarity, and guidance. By channeling the energy of Zonar during meditation or healing sessions, practitioners tap into a reservoir of ancient wisdom, guidance, and clarity that can be transformative.

HALU

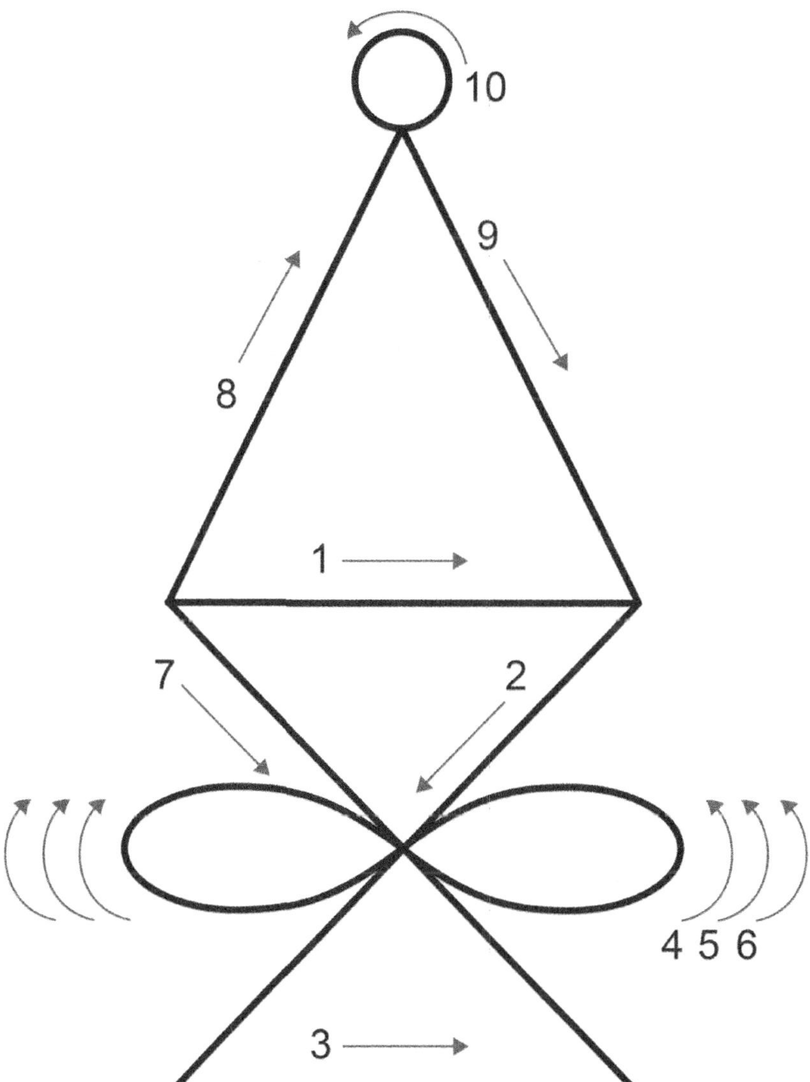

Introduced as the second symbol at the Karuna Reiki® level 1, Halu is not only a potent complement to Zonar but also powerful on its own. Its distinct ability to create a pyramid of energy embodies ancient wisdom and protection. This structure serves as both a shield from external negativity and a sanctuary of concentrated positivity, offering a transformative healing experience.

Halu has 3 main attributes:

- Provides strong psychic protection;
- Promotes self-acceptance and harmony through the healing of the emotional body;
- Connects to Archangel Raphael, the angel of healing;

Halu has the following uses:

- Acts as an inter-dimensional gateway toward the energy print of Archangel Raphael. This enables you to bring part of Raphael's healing energies into your life for physical support and deep emotional and spiritual introspection;
- Activate Halu on your palms and chakras. This symbol will help create a layer of energetic protection around your body through the constant use of the Reiki self-treatment;

- When used on the crown and third eye chakras, this symbol acts as a shield against psychic aggression and/or manipulation;
- Its structure forms a pyramid of energy that can surround a person, object, or group of people;
- Meditate on Halu to acknowledge your mistakes and avoid blaming others for your actions. Also, it enables you to harmonize with your imperfections and heal them through self-discipline and introspection;
- Use Cho Ku Rei + Sei He Ki + Hon Sha Ze Sho Nen + Zonar + Halu to send energy toward your past and help heal traumatic events, still present today;
- For room cleansing, consider using Zonar + Halu. Activate the sequence on the ceiling, walls, corners, floor, and center of the room. Together, they will help dissipate residual and negative energies;
- When activated on the primary chakras and their back projections, Halu creates an energetic armor of protection against malevolent intentions and energies;
- Use it during self-treatment to help reach the root of your mental and emotional imbalances, heal them, and continue your spiritual growth;
- Activate Halu + Zonar on your front and back to create a strong layer of energetic protection. This sequence will also provide a gradual energetic rejuvenating effect for the whole body;

HARTH

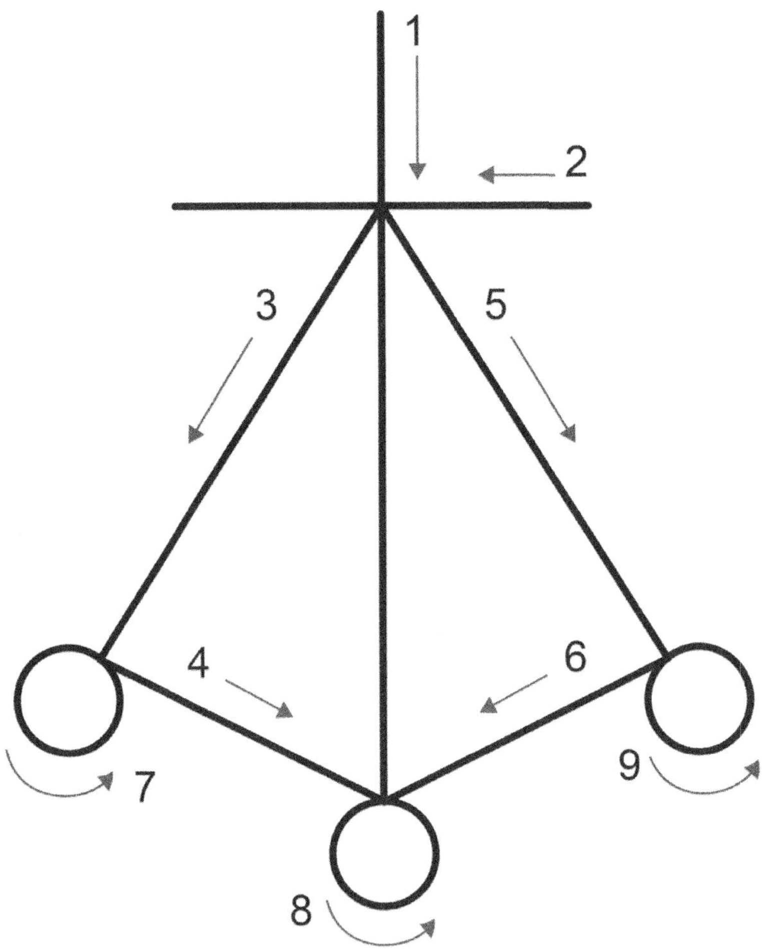

Harth is the 3rd symbol you learn at level 1 Karuna Reiki®. It's one of the highest vibrational symbols and represents pure compassion, love, and nourishment for the soul.

Harth has 3 main attributes:

- It acts as a gateway opener toward some of the purest manifestations of the universal life force energy;
- Enhances the energy flow of the upepr chakras;
- Helps heal the energetic structure of the soul - this can help prevent a number of cardiac problems;

Harth has the following uses:

- Before self-treatment, activate it on your palms and chakras, along with other Reiki symbols. This will enhance the flow and quality of energy through your body;
- It can be activated in the center of a room for a thorough, energetic cleansing. This will fill the space with compassion and love;
- By constantly activating Harth on the Soul Star and crown chakras, you enhance the opening of these two centers toward the divine, loving energies;

- Some practitioners claim that Harth opens the gateway toward Mother Mary. Others say it facilitates the connection with the Buddhist goddess Kwan Yin. This is possible because Harth helps establish a healthy relationship with the divine motherly energies;

- When sending energy toward your past, present, or future, add the Harth symbol. The energy of this symbol will help heal emotional imbalances related to the Yin (or feminine) side;

- The Sei He Ki + Shika Sei Ki + Harth sequences will help regenerate the essence of the soul. Activate it on your heart area and rest your palms there for about 10 minutes. This process will cleanse your soul, and you'll start feeling joyful and whole again;

- Harth works excellently with relationships, regardless of their nature. Use the Cho Ku Rei + Sei He Ki + Hon Sha Ze Sho Nen + Shika Sei Ki + Dai Ko Myo + Harth sequence toward that specific relationship. Channel energy for ~5-10 minutes each day for the greater good of that connection. This will cleanse the soul's essence of the people involved and help heal most of the emotional imbalances between them;

- Using Harth regularly in self-treatment can help prevent and/or even heal cardiac issues. Any imbalance at this level occurs because of an energetical breach and misunderstanding of a spiritual concept. In this case, the heart area is all about the ability to forgive, offer compassion and love;

- Harth helps us prevent and get rid of addictions, negative mental patterns, and habits. By using it in conjunction with Sei He Ki, Harth is an excellent mind resetter. It aids in freeing us from unnecessary residual energies;

- Regularly work with the Harth symbol to train yourself for emotional self-control;

Harth's essence lies in its incredible capacity to bridge the gaps in our spiritual and emotional selves. The very core of this symbol revolves around the universal truth that love and compassion are at the root of healing and personal growth. The powerful vibrations of Harth not only tend to the physical and energetic well-being but also foster a deep sense of inner peace and connection to the universe.

Further delving into its role in promoting connections with divine maternal energies, Harth offers a unique opportunity to rekindle our bond with nurturing and unconditional love. For those feeling disconnected or lost, it serves as a beacon, guiding them back to a space of warmth and belonging.

RAMA

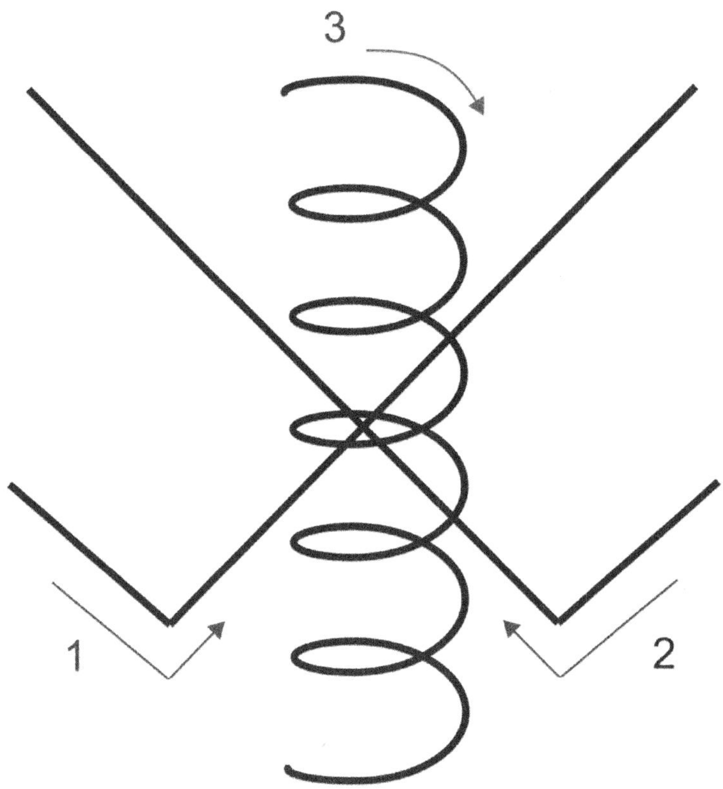

Rama is a strong symbol of cleansing and protection and the last one you learn at your first level of Karuna Reiki®.

Rama has 3 main attributes:

- Connects to the energy of Archangel Michael;
- It can be used for dissipating malevolent energies and entities from a person or a space;
- It can have a tremendous grounding effect;

Rama has the following uses:

- It can be activated on your palms and lower chakras, and therefore it can be used in the Reiki self-treatment. This will create an enhanced cleansing effect, especially over your inferior energetic fields - where most of our residual energy is stored;
- When activated in both the upper and lower corners as well as the center of a room, Rama removes low-vibrational entities and energies from that space. Also, consider drawing Rama above candles to amplify the purifying effect;
- For better grounding, activate Rama + Cho Ku Rei on each foot. Take it one step further and activate Rama on the first, second, and third chakras. Together, these actions will gradually help you

connect to the telluric energies, grounding you optimally;

- Rama is a good symbol for helping with temporary memory loss. Use Cho Ku Rei + Sei He Ki + Rama on the third eye chakra to enhance your ability to remember information;

- It serves as a gateway to the energy signature of Archangel Michael. This means that whenever you activate Rama, you call upon an extension of his energy;

- Activate Rama parallel to the ground and all around you. This will create strong protection against negative energies, malevolent intentions, and energetic vampires;

- Within the Reiki self-treatment, Rama will gradually release energetic blockages, especially the ones located in the lower part of your body;

- Activate Cho Ku Rei + Sei He Ki + Rama in front of you to open the energetic pathways toward your travels by removing any possible obstacles;

- Rama is an exceptional symbol for cleansing and protecting objects such as crystals, cars, wallets, purses, or anything that is of value to you;

- Consider activating Rama between you and a person to create a wall of energy through which no malevolent intentions will pass. However, be aware that this may affect the communication between the two of you. Add Cho Ku Rei to create an even stronger energy shield;

The profound essence of Rama lies in its ability to form a bridge between the earthly and the ethereal realms. Its connection to Archangel Michael, a divine protector, signifies its unmatched power in maintaining sanctity and purity in our spaces and souls. With life's challenges, be it energetic disturbances or emotional turbulences, Rama serves as an anchor, keeping us rooted and shielded from the storms.

GNOSA

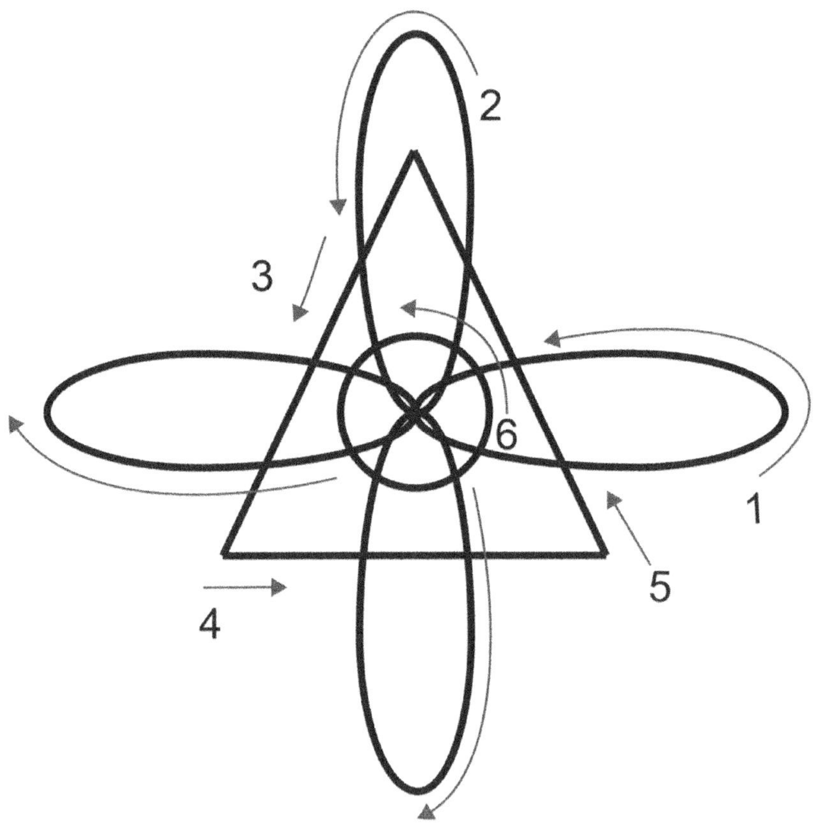

Gnosa is the first symbol you learn at Karuna level 2. It promotes "learning" as a concept, and was channeled by Reiki Master Marie Abraham.

Gnosa has 3 main attributes:

- It expands the mental field, therefore allowing the practitioner to accumulate more knowledge and wisdom;
- Helps you express and acknowledge the truth within a situation or conflict;
- It offers a better, easier connection to the higher self, developing your awareness;

Gnosa has the following uses:

- Before using Gnosa in your daily Reiki self-treatment, activate it on your palms and upper chakras (crown, third eye, throat, and heart) to gradually integrate the symbol's energy;
- When used between you and another person, it will bring to the surface any hidden thoughts or lies that could have been solved through simple communication. Additionally, if you activate it on your third eye chakra during a conversation, it can help you detect dishonesty;

- Gnosa helps you connect to the angels of wisdom. By using it regularly, you'll tap into your potential to reach a higher level of divine wisdom;

- Through meditation, this symbol can help you better connect to your higher self, therefore empowering you to grow from a spiritual standpoint by raising your consciousness;

- Activating a double Gnosa on the crown chakra can help alleviate fatigue, lethargy, and even aid in recovery from hangovers;

- When activated on a book or a course, Hon Sha Ze Sho Nen + Gnosa helps acknowledge and filter the received information so that it removes the chance of a faulty personal interpretation;

- Use the Cho Ku Rei + Sei He Ki + Gnosa sequence on the third eye chakra daily to enhance your ability to focus on specific tasks;

- This symbol also helps you gain mental clarity when it comes to expressing yourself through creative ventures. Activate Gnosa on the third eye and Gnosa + Shika So on the throat chakra. This will further improve your capability to express yourself through creativity and communication;

- Draw Gnosa above a book to facilitate the learning process. It's a way to connect to the author's thoughts and better understand what they were trying to convey;

- Gnosa works great in combination with most Reiki symbols. Its effect can be amplified in different ways, with different results. For example, Rama + Gnosa helps enhance physical strength | Gnosa + Dai Ko Myo on the crown chakra is for gaining a clearer understanding of the divine message and signs. Still, don't feel limited by these alone. Experiment with the various combinations that come to mind, and allow yourself to discover new and exciting patterns;

Gnosa pierces through the clouds of ignorance and unveils the wisdom that often lies dormant within us. In an era where information is vast and discerning truth from illusion is paramount, it acts as a guiding star. It reminds us that genuine learning is about mastering the core essence, not just accumulating meaningless data.

Gnosa stands as a bridge between intent and understanding, ensuring that our verbal or non-verbal messages resonate with clarity and authenticity. Embrace its teachings to navigate through life's complexities with sharp intuition and an open heart.

KRIYA

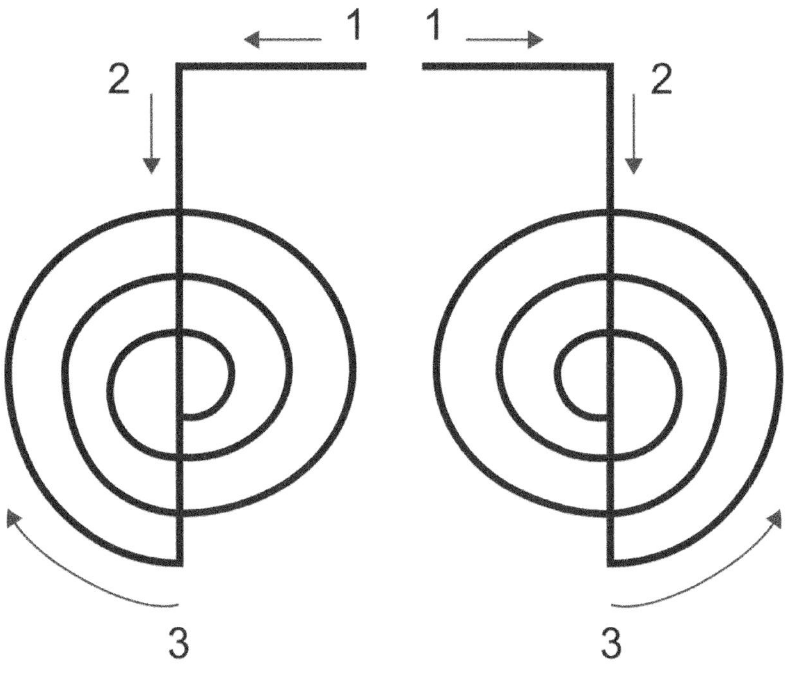

Kriya is the second symbol you learn at Karuna Reiki® level 2. It links the spiritual to the material world in terms of manifestation. Reiki Master Kathleen Milner channeled Kriya with the guidance of William Lee Rand, the founder of Karuna Reiki®.

Kriya has 3 main attributes:

- It helps bring your desires and goals into the material world;
- A symbol intended for healing the entire human race;
- It helps you connect to the angels of creativity;

Kriya has the following uses:

- Kriya can be activated on your palms and chakras before self-treatment. Using this symbol in your therapy will help you better integrate its energetic print;
- Use it to achieve an efficient grounding effect. Draw Kriya starting from the hips and continuing downwards toward your feet, where you'll finish with the spirals. Add Rama on each foot to create a solid grounding effect;
- This symbol connects to the angels of creativity. Use it in meditations and call upon those divine entities to

assist you in developing better skills and stimulate your creativity;

- Kriya is a very efficient symbol for Reiki projects. Consider adding it for a quicker manifestation of your goals. Remember that this manifests in the best way for each individual, so "quick" may vary from one person to another;

- When activated on the Soul Star and Crown chakras, Kriya can stimulate the physical manifestation of your goals if they are in accordance with the Divine will;

- Kriya has the power to help the entire human race. You can contribute by sending energy toward the whole planet for its greater good. To do so, use: Cho Ku Rei + Sei He Ki + Hon Sha Ze Sho Nen + Dai Ko Myo + Halu + Kriya. This sequence will create an optimal flow of energy designated for helping and healing humanity. Remember to limit this to no more than 10 minutes occasionally, and always conclude by adding "for everyone's greater good" at the end. Not everyone wants to change or to be healed, so we have to respect that!

- When activated on the third eye chakra, Kriya + Gnosa will amplify your ability to focus and remove mental obstacles that keep you from achieving your goals;

- Activate Kriya between you and a person to create an energy flow of harmony and understanding. You can use this method at a distance by adding Hon Sha Ze Sho Nen;

- If you use crystals in your therapy sessions or Reiki projects, you can apply Kriya + Cho Ku Rei to your crystals. Your intention should be to manifest your desires and goals into the physical world. This will focus the energy on that particular outcome;

- Kriya is a symbol that offers many features and attributes. Unfortunately, some of these are not yet known by most practitioners. Therefore, meditating on this symbol and integrating it into your life can reveal new and exciting ways of using its energy;

Kriya serves as a bridge between our dreams and reality, acting as a vessel for the manifestation of our deepest desires. This potent symbol reminds us that we are co-creators of the universe.

Furthermore, the essence of Kriya goes beyond personal ambitions. At its core, it embodies the universal yearning for growth, enlightenment, and harmony. When we reach out to the angels of creativity, we tap into an ageless reservoir of inspiration and vision. It not only refines our individual pursuits but also equips us to make positive contributions to the collective consciousness.

IAVA (Java)

Reiki Master Catherine Mills channeled Iava, the third symbol you learn at your Karuna level 2 training. It symbolizes the 4 main elements (water, air, fire, and earth) required for life. It's highly effective for lifting the veil of illusions, negative patterns, and deceit.

Iava has 3 main attributes:

- Connects you to the angels of harmony and nature;
- Assists in dissolving misconceptions and illusions;
- Helps you cultivate the ideal reality for your current energy level;

Iava has the following uses:

- Activate Iava on the palms and chakras before self-treatment to help balance the primordial elements that influence your body's health state;
- Iava serves as a gateway to the angels of harmony, allowing you to continuously send energy and seek their guidance;
- By activating a double Iava symbol on the crown chakra, you can achieve optimal mental balance and guard against harmful thought patterns;

- With its ability to dismantle deceit, Iava aids in discerning the truth in any event, situation, or narrative. Activate Iava between yourself and another person to uncover their genuine intentions;

- Keep in mind that regular use of this symbol can shed many of your existing preconceptions. Iava "rewires" the brain to eliminate unnecessary patterns, superstitions, and other unhealthy thoughts;

- Iava + Sei He Ki can help erase the energy imprint of patterns leading to addiction, depending on an individual's willingness to change;

- Send energy toward the future using the Cho Ku Rei + Sei He Ki + Hon Sha Ze Sho Nen + Iava sequence to guard against malevolent influences and harmful patterns;

SHANTI

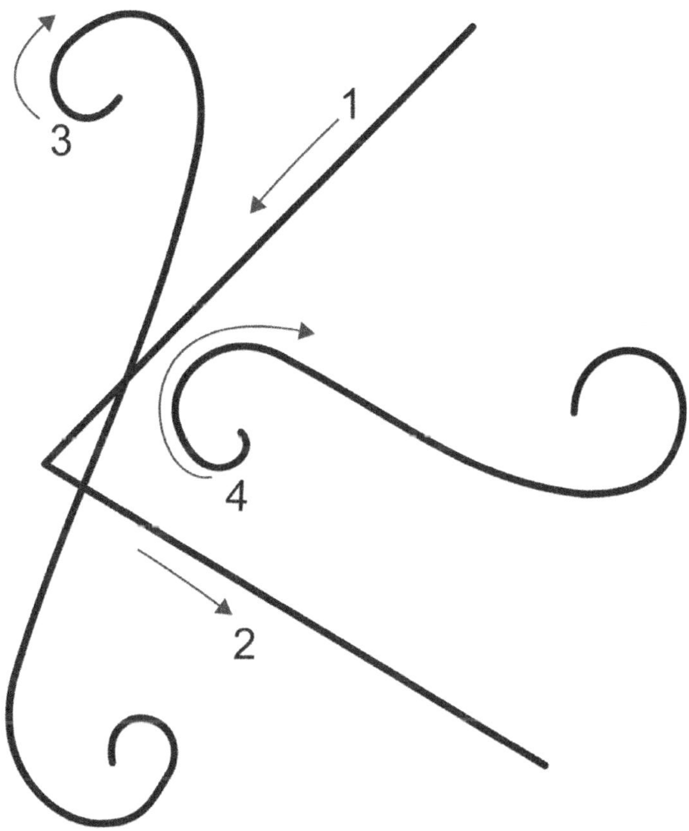

Shanti is the fourth and last symbol that you learn at your level 2 Karuna training. Shanti was channeled by Reiki Master Pat Courtney, and it represents the key to peaceful energy.

Shanti has 3 main attributes:

- Shanti is one of the few symbols in Reiki that helps heal past emotional traumas directly;
- It also helps remove negative emotions from the present, such as stress, depression, or anxiety;
- Whether used in self-treatment or meditation, Shanti brings the energy of peace into your life;

Shanti has the following uses:

- Activate it on your palms and upper chakras (the crown, third eye, throat, and heart chakras) during self-treatment to enhance the flow of the universal life force energy and promote peace;
- Because Shanti is a high-vibrational symbol, it can heal past and present emotional traumas when used regularly in self-treatment. The healing process involves acceptance and detachment from the negative energies caused by traumas;

- Regularly activating Shanti on the Soul Star chakra during self-treatment will help enhance your connection to your spirit guides;

- Shanti can help open the third eye chakra (not the third eye). This symbol clears our residual and negative energies from this area, allowing the energetic center to gradually open in time. Add Gnosa and your intuition to support your ability to assimilate information;

- This symbol acts as a key that opens the gateway for the entities of peace and spiritual guidance. Therefore, meditating on this symbol will enable you to connect to the vibrations of these divine entities. The best part is that if you connect to these entities regularly, they can even become your own Reiki guides;

- When placed in the center of a room, Shanti will bring harmony and peace to that space. Add Sei He Ki for an amplified effect;

- Through its continuous use, Shanti has the ability to counter the effects of depression, anxiety, and stress. Also, it's a great remedy for people who suffer from insomnia;

- When applied to the throat chakra, our communication becomes harmonious and clear;

- If activated in the heart area, Shanti provides a feeling of peace and relaxation deep within our soul. Add Sei He Ki + Shika Sei Ki + Harth for an enhanced effect;

- Many mantras and sutras include the word Shanti because of its ability to promote peace. You just have to find the ones that resonate with you;

Shanti's very essence is rooted in the word "peace." It embodies serenity, calm, and the absence of disturbance. Embrace this symbol to radiate these attributes outward, influencing those around you and the spaces you occupy.

Shanti stands out as a holistic enhancer, offering a comprehensive approach to well-being. This is because the heart of Shanti is: “balance.” Every time you use this symbol, you invite balance into your life, striving to strike the proper equilibrium between your inner and outer worlds.

OM (AUM)

This is the last and most powerful symbol, which belongs to the master level or the third Karuna Reiki® level. OM is an ancient Sanskrit symbol that bridges our inner Divine energy and the Universal life force energy.

OM has 3 main attributes:

- It is a permanent link to the purest manifestation of the life force energy;
- Through meditation, it stimulates spiritual awakening;
- It also nourishes the heart and mind with pure energy;

OM has the following uses:

- To significantly enhance the flow of the universal life force energy, prior to the Reiki self-treatment, OM can be activated on the palms and superior chakras. Additionally, you can do the same for the Soul Star, crown, third eye, throat, and heart chakras;
- Activate OM + Shika Sei Ki + Harth in the heart area to support the energy flow and cleanse the soul of residual and negative elements;
- When used consistently on the Soul Star, crown, and third eye chakras, OM helps foster higher awareness and instills a sense of gratitude toward life. Its vibration will also provide a feeling of self-sufficiency;

- When used on the throat area, OM enables you to express your emotions and thoughts harmoniously. Add Shika So to further intensify the effect;

- OM connects to the angels of Divine harmony. These are some of the highest vibrational entities in existence. This means it can bring their energy into our lives and help raise our consciousness;

- Whenever activated in the center of the room, OM will bring calmness and harmony while providing a solid cleansing effect;

- Meditating on this symbol will gradually change the energetic structure of the brain by dissolving negative thoughts and patterns;

- Cho Ku Rei + Sei He Ki + Hon Sha Ze Sho Nen + Dai Ko Myo + OM will connect to the highest, purest manifestation of the universal life force energy. This sequence can be used on the crown chakra to (re)activate the connection to the light. You can also apply it in the center of a room or on the ceiling to create a powerful cone of light;

- OM or AUM is the source of all existing sounds and the echo of the divine creation. When used in the mantra "Om Mani Padme Hum", its vibration is amplified. There are quite a few versions of this mantra, and each of them has the ability to cleanse a space when chanted or played as a mantra;

- While this symbol has a rather abstract meaning in Hindu philosophy, in Karuna, its energy print is related to spiritual ascension and evolution through awareness;

- You can also print it alongside other Reiki symbols and display the framed symbols next to you in the workplace or at home for a constant flow of pure energy;

The vibration produced by chanting OM is believed to resonate with the natural rhythm of the universe, promoting inner peace and aligning the self with cosmic energies. When you integrate OM into your Reiki practice, you embrace centuries of spiritual wisdom.

As you continue to work with OM, it's worth reflecting on its ancient roots and considering how its singular sound can unify thoughts, balance energies, and bring about a profound sense of wholeness. Through this understanding, your connection with OM becomes a journey through time and consciousness.

Shamballa Reiki Symbols

John Armitage, better known as Hari Das Melchizedek, introduced the Shamballa Multi-Dimensional Healing Reiki System to our world. Although it initially aimed to mirror the original Usui Reiki system, Shamballa Reiki evolved to become more complex.

Shamballa Reiki unlocks some of the most potent energies, symbols, and meditation techniques within the Reiki realm. However, this doesn't mean it's more complete or superior to others. It simply functions at a higher vibrational frequency.

How To Go About It

My recommended path is to first progress through Usui and Karuna Reiki®.

While Usui primarily addresses physical and mental well-being, Karuna delves deeper into emotional and spiritual healing. Shamballa Reiki takes you even further, elevating your consciousness and spiritual growth. It expands your awareness and surfaces karmic debts that need settling for spiritual growth to occur. This system essentially 'accelerates' the spiritual growth process, providing a clear path forward.

Some may find this concept appealing, while others may shy away. It all depends on your personal objectives and your desired progression.

With that said, it's important to recognize that beyond its healing attributes, Shamballa Reiki primarily serves as a system for spiritual ascension.

About The Symbols

Despite their complexity and high vibrational nature, there's limited information available on most Shamballa Reiki symbols. While some characteristics are well-defined, much remains to be discovered. The system contains over 350 symbols, each revealed only when the practitioner is deemed ready and wise enough to harness their potential.

The Tale Behind Shamballa

It is said that the system originates from Atlantis, the legendary sunken continent. That population was incredibly advanced from a technological and spiritual standpoint. However, the thirst for power eventually began to show and quickly sabotage one another. This led to excessive greed, hate, and, ultimately, conflict. The continent was sunk as a "punishment" for failing to manage and control their divine-offered talents and gifts. Alongside the incarnation of Count of Saint Germain at that time, a few fellow priests known as the "Inspirers" managed to flee to the area known today as Tibet. They attempted to teach the locals a select few of these secret and sacred symbols. But greed and lust for power settled once again among the inhabitants. Thus, Saint Germain and the Inspirers kept most symbols secret and offered wisdom, teachings, and spiritual tokens only to those who proved worthy over time. It is said that some of the Inspirers were behind the secret methods of constructing the pyramids of Egypt and Central America, while others were offering their wisdom in some areas of Asia, laying the groundwork for future civilizations to emerge.

Even if this tale may sound farfetched, the lesson is that some things are hidden from us so that we do not misuse them for our own selfish, greedy ends. We receive what best suits us only when we are wise and disciplined. As mentioned, this complex system reveals only a few symbols, with little information available. Through dedicated research, meditation, and practice, I've gathered as much information as I've been permitted to receive up to this point.

MER KA FA KA LISH MA

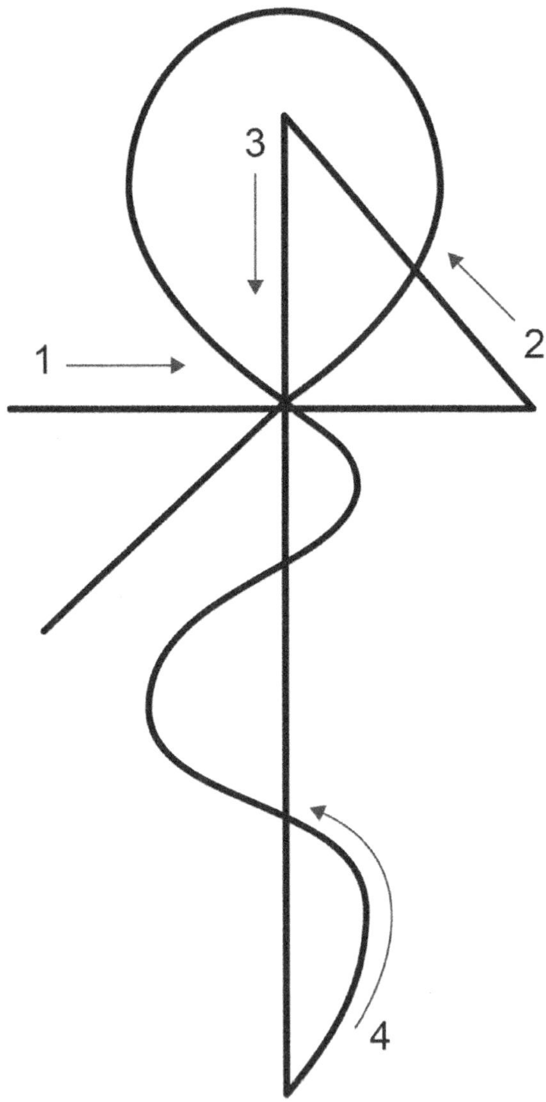

Mer Ka Fa Ka Lish Ma belongs to the second level of Shamballa Reiki. At first glance, you'll probably notice it resembles the Egyptian cross. This is no coincidence, as ancient civilizations possessed vast esoteric knowledge about energy, healing, and the universe. Drawing on this energy means tapping into centuries of wisdom and understanding that transcends the everyday experience.

Mer Ka Fa Ka Lish Ma has 3 main attributes:

- It can activate the inert DNA sequences in a slow, gradual way that is optimum for each practitioner;
- Helps cleanse the soul energy essence;
- Helps restore the energetic health and physical structure of any organ;

Mer Ka Fa Ka Lish Ma has the following uses:

- You can activate Mer Ka Fa Ka Lish Ma on your palms and upper chakras (Soul Star and crown chakras) prior to self-treatment. This will bring an enhanced level of energy flow as well as integrate the energy print of this symbol into your body;
- The constant use of this symbol will gradually change the structure of your DNA, meaning that some of the inert sequences could become active. This will enable you to discover new spiritual potentials;

- In meditation or prior to the Reiki self-treatment, you can activate this symbol on your wrists. This stimulates the process of activating new DNA sequences;

- You can draw this symbol on the front and back of your body. Doing this will align your chakras and remove residual energies;

- This symbol has a strong connection to our planet's beneficial, nurturing, motherly energies. Activate it on both sides of the body before the Reiki self-treatment. This will enable you to become an efficient channel that unites the universal life force energy with the Earth's vital energy;

- Mer Ka Fa Ka Lish Ma will also help gradually raise the Kundalini energy that resides in the sacral area. That's because, among many other things, this symbol represents the evolution of Kundalini from its dormant stage to fully awakened and aware;

- An enhanced regenerating effect can be created by using Mer Ka Fa Ka Lish Ma + Zonar + Halu on an affected body area. Together, they offer the necessary energy required to restructure an integral part of a tissue or organ;

- Antahkarana and Mer Ka Fa Ka Lish Ma are an ideal combination for deeply cleansing your mental, emotional, and energetic bodies. Simply activating them in a room will gradually change its vibration;

- Mer Ka Fa Ka Lish Ma has a powerful beneficial energy that can help cleanse a place of malevolent entities. Just activate it on the ceiling and in the center of a room alongside the rest of the Reiki symbols;

- Keep in mind that this is one of the symbols that has the potential to create life-changing effects. Constantly exposing yourself to this symbol can help you connect to your inner self and higher consciousness. It's a process that will gradually lead your spiritual evolution;

Mer Ka Fa Ka Lish Ma serves as a token for spiritual ascension through its ability to touch on deep DNA healing. This practice fundamentally rejuvenates our essence. When you invoke Mer Ka Fa Ka Lish Ma, you are harnessing Earth's nurturing energies, intertwining with the universe's life force, and grounding yourself in the process.

ANTAHKARANA

It is said that Antahkarana dates back thousands of years and that it was later adopted by Hindu and Buddhist cultures. It represents an esoteric and philosophical concept based on healing the subconscious. This makes it one of the most interesting and powerful symbols in existence.

Antahkarana has 3 main attributes:

- It balances your body from a mental, emotional, and energetic perspective;
- Helps create and/or restore the connection between the subconscious and the higher self;
- Even when simply placed next to you, it activates and purifies your chakras;

Antahkarana has the following uses:

- It can be drawn on your palms like the rest of the Reiki symbols and then applied to all chakras. Antahkarana will offer a considerable enhancement in the flow of the universal life force energy;
- Keeping a printed version close to you, whether at home or your workplace, will stimulate the flow of vital energy through your body;
- Using or placing it near you will also cleanse the connection between your inner self (subconscious) and your higher self (divine consciousness). This will enable

you to gradually link the two elements and grow your awareness and consciousness;

- The Yin Antahkarana is very useful in healing emotional imbalances and helps activate the upper chakras. The Yang Antahkarana helps amplify your energetic fields and vital energy. It resonates with the lower chakras and balances the Yin-Yang energies in your body;

- The Antahkarana symbol helps you boost your immunity and focus. This process takes place by cleansing your mind and energetic fields of residual thoughts and energies;

- When activated on the crown chakra and then guided through the rest of the body, Antahkarana creates a vortex of energy that has a powerful energetic cleansing effect;

- Meditating on this symbol will enable you to free your mind of negative thoughts. This will gradually raise your awareness and cleanse the mental, emotional, and spiritual layers of your body;

- When placed within a room, Antahkarana can transform negative energies into positive ones and deter malevolent entities. The ideal version for this action is the Antahkarana Cross;

- A square pattern featuring 16 Antahkaranas can also help remove negative energies and amplify the flow of the universal life force energy. You can place it on a wall or under any piece of furniture, including your bed;

- Antahkarana has a purifying effect on crystals, food, water, and anything organic. Keep this in mind when you decide to buy and place crystals in your home;

Antahkarana Yang stimulates and promotes a robust flow of life force energy, primarily nurturing the lower chakras - the Solar Plexus, Sacral, and Root. These chakras are fundamental to our sense of stability, confidence, and connection to the physical world.

Antahkarana Yin harmonizes the flow through the upper chakras - the Crown, Third Eye, Throat, and Heart. These chakras govern our connection to the universe, intuition, communication, and love.

Antahkarana bridges the inner self to the higher self, helping you become aware of the potentials and imbalances you may need to address through energy work.

MOTOR ZANON

Motor Zanon is part of Shamballa Reiki level 2. It's like having a spiritual antibiotic in your healing toolkit. While many understand the physical aspects of bacteria and infections, few recognize the energy print they possess. Its unique capability to recalibrate and fortify the energy within is a testament to its invaluable role in Shamballa Reiki. By regularly tapping into its essence, you're healing the present and laying the groundwork for your future well-being.

Embracing Motor Zanon's energy is like setting up a protective shield, ensuring that your vibrational frequency remains harmonious and robust against any disruptions.

Motor Zanon has 3 main attributes:

- Helps remove the negative energy of bacteria, infections, and viruses;
- Restores the energetic structure within the affected area;
- Attracts healing entities that offer protection to the affected area;

Motor Zanon has the following uses:

- It can be activated within your palms before self-treatment. This will help you better integrate its energy into your body and support a strong immune system over time. There's no specific need to activate this symbol on the chakras;

- Activate 3 x Cho Ku Rei + 3 x Motor Zanon + 3 x Cho Ku Rei on an infection. Keep your hands above that area for about 10 minutes. This sequence will remove the negative energy of the condition and generate the necessary healing vibration;

- Repeat the process 3 times/day;

- Motor Zanon accesses protective entities that guard against bacteria, viruses, and infections. Meditating on this symbol will help raise your vibration, thus creating a layer of protection against lower-vibrational energies that come with bacteria and infections;

HO KA O ILI ILI

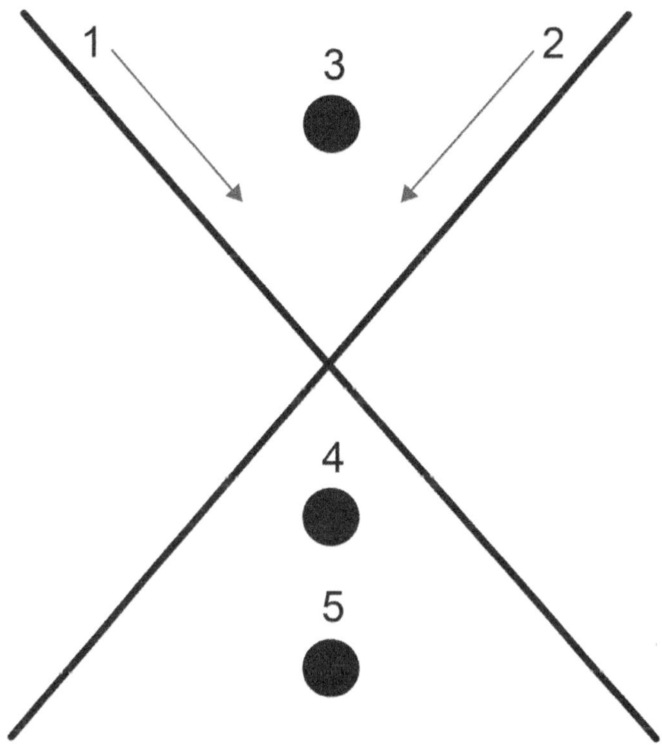

Ho Ka O Ili Ili is part of level 3 Shamballa Reiki, standing for respect, appreciation, and honor.

Ho Ka O Ili Ili has 3 main attributes:

- It creates an aura of respect around you;
- Helps boost self-confidence;
- Creates a protective layer when combined with other Reiki symbols;

Ho Ka O Ili Ili has the following uses:

- Activate it in your palms, on the crown chakra, and on your front, back, left, and right. This will help bring the energy of respect and self-trust;
- Using the same procedure, activate the following sequence: Cho Ku Rei + Sei He Ki + Ho Ka O Ili Ili to create an aura of protection around you. It acts as a shield against those with disrespectful intentions or negative projections;
- When activated above the crown chakra, it enhances the flow of the universal life force energy;
- One lesser-known combination is activating the Dragon Of Fire + Ho Ka O Ili Ili in front of you. You can use it when you want to send back any malevolent thoughts and intentions to the person who sent them

toward you. However, exercise caution when using this method;

- Integrate its energy within your structures by using it regularly in self-treatment;

Working with Ho Ka O Ili Ili resembles weaving a mantle of dignity around yourself. It's like harnessing an energy that immediately commands respect, not out of arrogance, but genuine self-worth. It serves as a reminder of our intrinsic value, strengthening our internal foundation of self-belief. Use it to cultivate a healthy relationship with yourself, reinforcing the idea that respect goes beyond how others see us but how we perceive ourselves.

ABUNDANCE SYMBOL

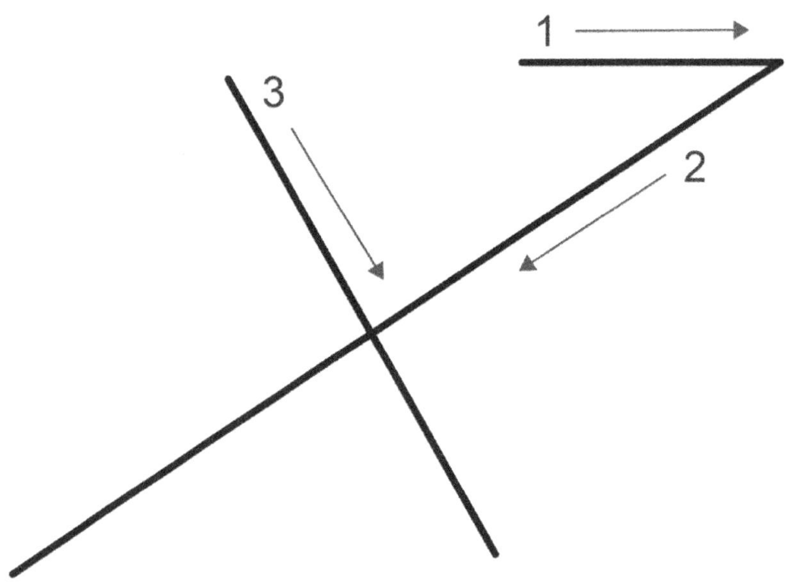

You get introduced to the Abundance symbol at level 3, Shamballa Reiki. It's an ideal spiritual tool for enabling practitioners to create a holistic approach to prosperity where an overflow of love, health, happiness, and inner peace come together.

Abundance has 3 main attributes:

- Attracts the energy of abundance on all levels - physical, emotional, and spiritual;
- Unlocks the potential flow of prosperity within your life;
- Teaches harmonious management of income from both physical and spiritual standpoints;

Abundance has the following uses:

- It can be activated on your palms and crown chakra prior to self-treatment to help you integrate its energy into your life;
- The Abundance symbol is extremely beneficial in your Reiki projects, and its power is amplified by other Reiki symbols;
- When sending energy to your future, use Cho Ku Rei + Sei He Ki + Hon Sha Ze Sho Nen + Abundance. This will gradually unlock the potential for manifesting abundance on all levels;

- Print out the symbol and place it on a wall, under your work desk, or wherever your intuition guides you. This way, you will gradually bring the energy of abundance and prosperity to that room;

The Abundance symbol dissolves spiritual and energetic blockages that have prevented your progress in the past. It dispels the limited beliefs and fears you might have accumulated about wealth and invites a sense of acceptance that prosperity isn't just about collecting but also about giving, sharing, and wisely utilizing your resources.

PALM MASTER

You receive access to the energy of Palm Master at level 3 Shamballa Reiki, a symbol that elegantly bridges the connection between the inner self, soul, and the higher self.

Palm Master has 3 main attributes:

- Enhances the connection between the inner self (kundalini), the soul (divine spark), and the higher self (connection with the divine);
- Establishes a connection over time between the pineal and pituitary glands;
- Enables you to become a perfect channel through which the earth and divine energy flow;

Palm Master has the following uses:

- Activate it on your palms and the full length of your body's front side prior to self-treatment. This will enhance the flow of the universal life force energy and help you blend with the symbol's vibration. To amplify the effect, visualize it on the full length of your body's backside as well;
- Because this symbol acts as a whole when activated on the entire body, it stimulates a series of events at the energetic level. It helps activate the crown chakra, establishes a connection between the pineal and pituitary gland, and activates the primary chakras for grounding;

- The bond, which Palm Master strengthens between the pineal and pituitary glands, serves as a conduit for elevated awareness, opening channels to heightened spiritual insights. This connection fosters a sense of unity with the universe and empowers the practitioner to navigate life with more profound intuition and understanding.

- It stimulates the Soul Star chakra and enables you to become a perfect channel between the telluric and divine energies;

- The constant use of this high-vibrational symbol helps raise your awareness of yourself and the world around you. This leads to an expansion of consciousness and gradual spiritual growth;

AMSUI

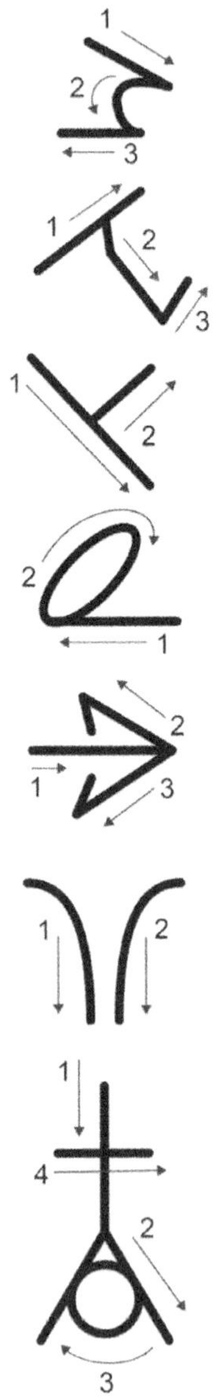

At Shamballa level 3, you gain access to the Amsui Reiki symbol, channeled by Bas Van Woelderen. While Amsui comprises 7 smaller symbols, it functions as a singular energetic structure.

Amsui has 3 main attributes:

- Predominantly used in attunements, Amsui helps balance your energetic structures, allowing your body to more effectively receive universal energy;
- It symbolizes completion, unity and the spiritual pillar between heaven and earth, providing the essential elements for spiritual evolution;
- Breaks the patterns of negative programs that we encounter in our life;

Amsui has the following uses:

- Unlike many Reiki symbols, Amsui doesn't necessarily need to be activated on the palms. Instead, you can activate it on the front side of the body before self-treatment to distribute the energy throughout the body harmoniously. Each of its 7 elements corresponds to a chakra;
- Activate Amsui in the middle of a room to dismantle any negative programs that might be present and bring a sense of unity and peace;

- Activated on the crown chakra before meditation or self-treatment, Amsui will help integrate its energy and promote emotional balance;

- Activating the Cho Ku Rei + Sei He Ki + Hon Sha Ze Sho Nen + Amsui sequence on your crown chakra can help dissolve negative patterns and programs;

- Amsui has a strong connection with Archangel Michael. Draw it above your dominant hand to activate Michael's sword, and use it to cut negative or residual strings attached to your chakras or dissolve negative projections from other people;

- Tap into Amsui's vibration through meditation for overall balance and to connect to your soul's energy of peace and integrity;

Symbols From Other Systems

Many different systems of Reiki have emerged from the shared knowledge of numerous Reiki Masters and spiritual devotees. These systems often feature high-vibrational symbols that we can use to support our energetic bodies.

Remember that symbols serve as keys, unlocking the potential of the universal life force energy. Therefore, each symbol holds its unique benefit, making it useful in various therapeutic contexts and for diverse purposes. However, there is no universal way of healing. In fact, you're the critical element that can support any method in most situations. By channeling the universal energy, the potential to trigger change is in your control. So, deciding which symbol to use for different results is up to you.

That's why I feel it's necessary to introduce symbols beyond the traditionally known Reiki systems that you can integrate into your practice, regardless of your attunements. Their mere existence can elevate your vibration levels. Some belong to other spiritual practices or systems, while others are standalone elements that represent esoteric and philosophical concepts.

When you understand a symbol and begin to use it regularly, its energy and information will become part of your daily existence. This interaction could be perceived as an "initiation" into the symbol or the practice it represents. However, it largely depends on your vibration and your resonance with the symbol or practice.

NOTE: *The symbols below are presented in no specific order but have clear descriptions and practical benefits.*

IMPORTANT: *Always seek consent before using a symbol on someone else, and ensure an ethical practice!*

HOSANNA – VI

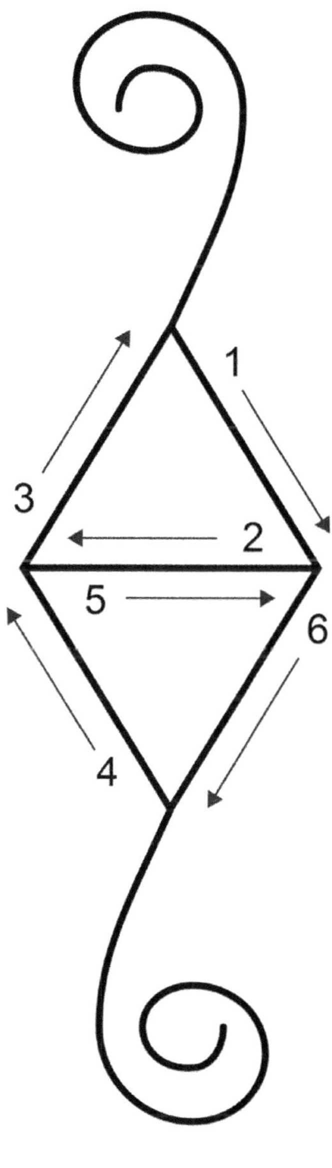

HOSANNA – V2

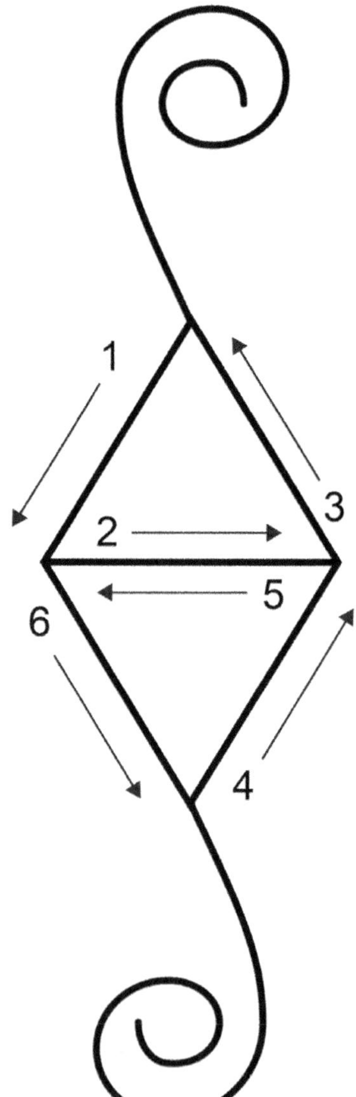

While initially associated with the Karuna Reiki® system, Hosanna, channeled by Reiki Master Eileen Gurhy, is not officially recognized as part of it.

Hosanna has 3 main attributes:

- Removes inner blockages that prevent your goals from manifesting;
- Helps cleanse a room energetically;
- You can activate it in two ways depending on your intention and needs;

Hosanna has the following uses:

- You can integrate this symbol within your Reiki practice by activating it on your palms and crown chakra prior to self-treatment. Hosanna will enhance the energy flow and create a harmonious vibration;
- Hosanna is ideal in releasing mental, emotional, and energetic blockages while providing a calming and cleansing effect. You can do this through the Cho Ku Rei + Sei He Ki + Hosanna sequence of symbols;
- Hosanna is strongly connected to the vibration of Archangel Michael and Count of Saint Germain. You can invoke them whenever you wish to use this symbol to enhance its cleansing abilities;

- The second version has a more direct use, meaning you can apply it to a specific imbalance with the assistance of Archangel Michael and the Count of Saint Germain;

- Display Hosanna in your workplace or at home to benefit from its influence. Channel energy toward the symbol for 5-10 minutes regularly to help remove procrastination and mental blockages;

- Hosanna can potentially create harmony between Yin and Yang energies;

- Use Hosanna in distance healing and addressing past traumas. Activate the Cho Ku Rei + Sei He Ki + Hon Sha Ze Sho Nen + Hosanna sequence on your palms and open a dimension toward distance, past, or future. Send energy for 10 minutes two times per week to help dissolve the energies that keep you stuck;

JOHRE (JOHREI)

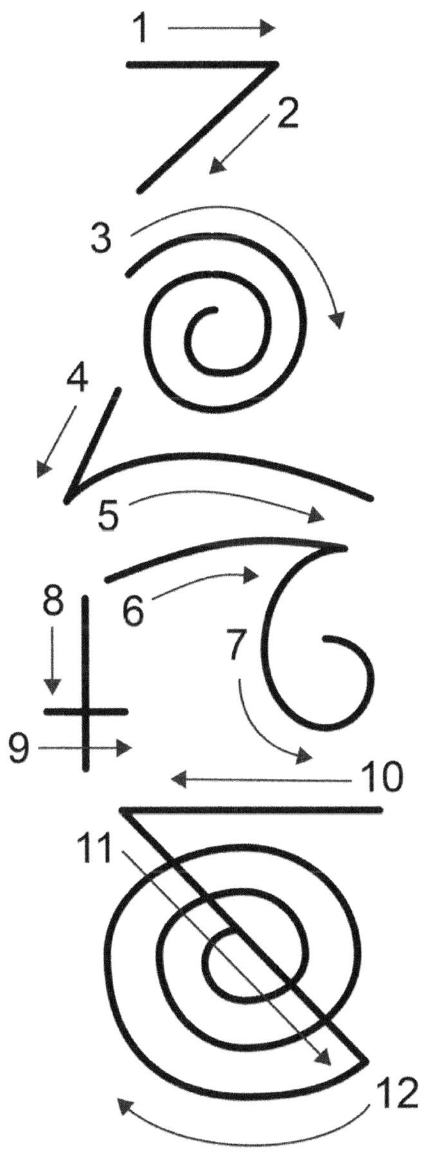

Johre is both a spiritual practice and a form of energy, similar to Reiki's vibration, balancing the Yin and Yang energies. Reiki represents Yin, while Johre represents Yang. Its origins can be traced back to Japan, and it roughly translates to "purification of the spirit through light."

Johre has 3 main attributes:

- Removes unnecessary, residual energies;
- Brings pure energy to your chakras and activates them;
- Emanates high-vibrational energy when placed in a room and balances the Yin and Yang energies;

Johre has the following uses:

- Johre corresponds to the crown and Soul Star chakras. Visualize it before self-treatment to facilitate a better flow of energy through your body;
- It directly influences your spiritual growth. Through constant exposure, you increase your potential of clearing negative and residual energies while gradually raising your awareness and consciousness levels;
- One useful practice is to place this symbol near you or hang it on a wall. I personally have a drawing by a calligraphy aficionado that radiates an energy beam optimal for my growth. Best of all, it won't force change, but rather, it will facilitate the necessary

environment that provides you with the required awareness for healing;

- Johre School of Healing claims that the layout of this symbol enables it to emanate over 2500 photons of light. It might sound abstract, but what's important is that it can bring healing with its simple presence;
- Johre acts as a direct link to your Reiki spirit guides, "specialized" in emotional and spiritual healing. Having this symbol around will facilitate your connection to these divine entities through meditation;

LON SAY

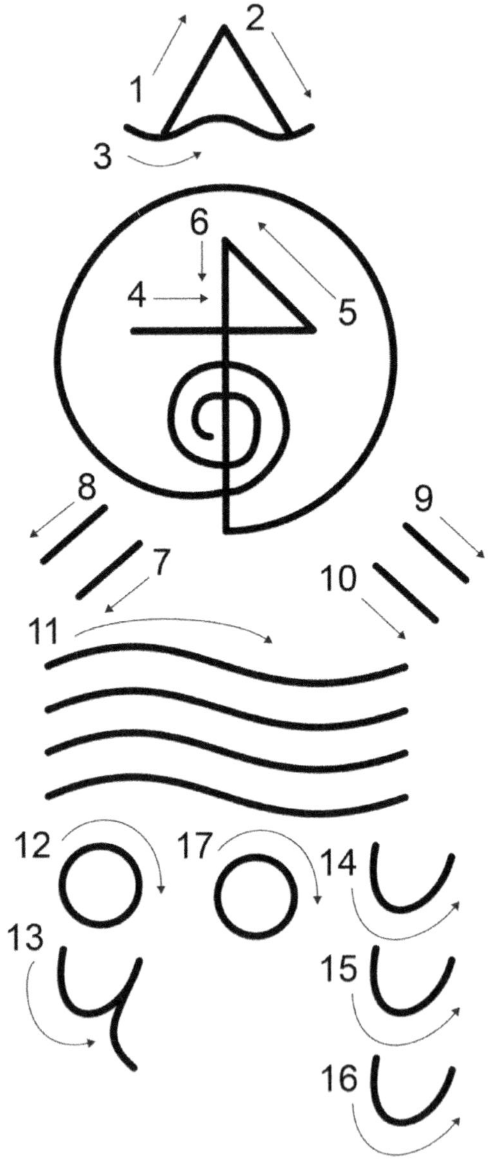

This symbol, believed to have Tibetan origins, has one notable feature: it aids in removing infections and supports the body's self-healing mechanism. Specifically, it provides the necessary vibration to remove the negative energy that supports infections and bacteria.

Lon Say has the following uses:

- Cho Ku Rei + Sei He Ki + Motor Zanon + Lon Say sequence facilitates an easy, quick, and smooth healing process. Lon Say + Motor Zanon make the perfect "team" for disintegrating the negative energy that comes with infections, viruses, or bacteria;
- It's effective in warding off malevolent energies and specific negative entities;
- I believe further uses can be discovered through meditation and practice;

ANTI-CANCER

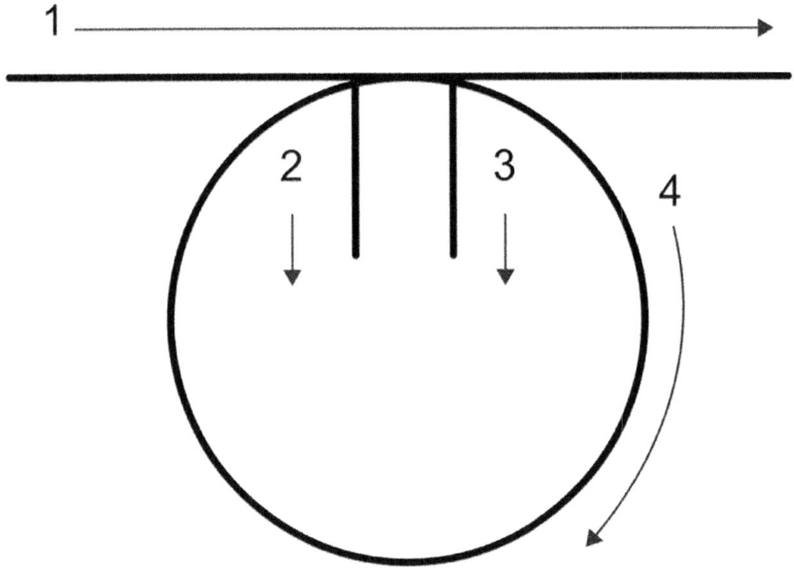

Attributed to the Shamballa Reiki system, this symbol was channeled by Loril Moondream, an affiliate of the White Mountain Apache tribe.

Anti-Cancer has the following attribute:

- Slows the spread and multiplication of cancer cells by disintegrating their specific energies;

" The inability to forgive is the number one spiritual cause of most cancers.

Given its high vibration, this symbol prompts the concept of "forgiveness" in a patient's mind, emphasizing its importance.

One must offer forgiveness to oneself and then to others.

Anti-Cancer has the following uses:

The best way to use the Anti-Cancer symbol is to activate it above the crown chakra and "push it" through the physical body to stimulate the development of healthy cells while inhibiting the growth of malignant/tumorous cells.

CHO KU RET

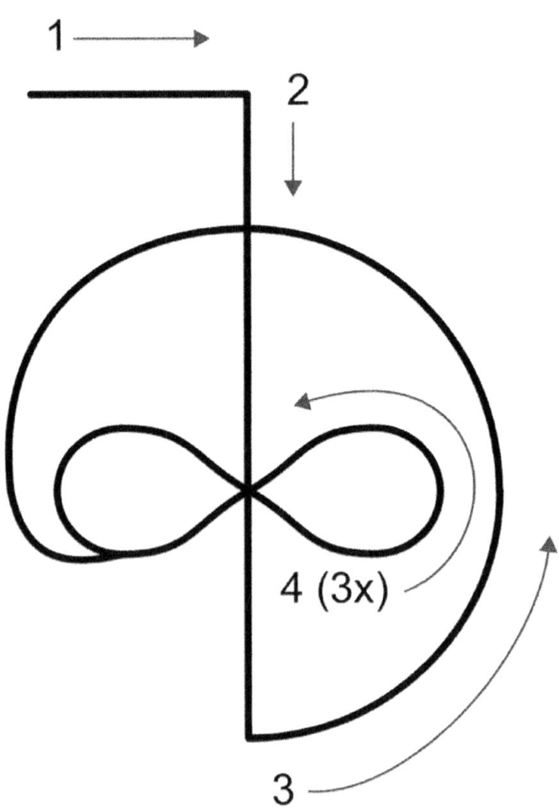

Just as Cho Ku Rei serves as the power symbol in the Usui Reiki system, Cho Ku Ret holds that role in the Seichim Reiki system.

Cho Ku Ret has 3 main attributes:

- Cleanses and removes residual energies wherever it is applied;
- Activates chakras and enhances the properties of other Reiki symbols;
- Creates energetic motion in entities that are non-cellular;

Cho Ku Ret has the following uses:

- Activate it on your palms and chakras prior to the Reiki self-treatment to amplify the flow of the universal life force energy;
- A distinctive feature of Cho Ku Ret is its ability to stimulate energy flow and cleanse non-biological structures, such as computers, cars, and machinery. While not "alive" in a traditional sense, these objects include spiritual elements, like entities and energy imprints, that can impact us;
- Cho Ku Ret can stimulate the energy flow through meridian points, where the energy can stagnate.

Visualize a small Cho Ku Ret where the meridians intersect to release and enhance the energy flow;

- Activate Cho Ku Ret on a specific organ (e.g., the liver or heart) to stimulate the vital energy flow through its meridians and help heal its energetic structure. Doing so will initiate the healing process by flooding the organ with pure light;

- Though they share many functions, Cho Ku Ret operates at a slightly higher vibration compared to Cho Ku Rei;

- To release a person from negative or residual energies, apply Cho Ku Ret on the body's anterior and posterior areas;

- Draw Cho Ku Ret on each wall, ceiling, floor, corner, and center of a room for general cleansing. Add the rest of the Reiki symbols to enable a "vortex" of beneficial energies through that space;

REIKI HARMONY

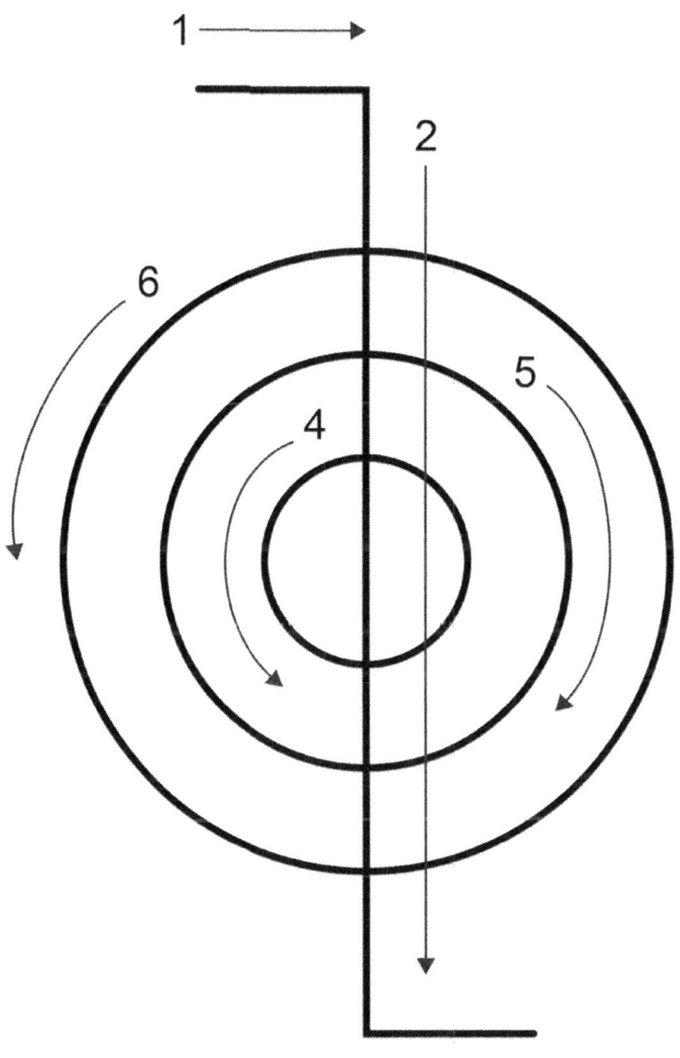

While this symbol doesn't belong to a specific Reiki system, it's regarded as a "neo-Reiki" totem for harmony and peace.

Harmony has 3 main attributes:

- Brings harmony wherever it is activated or placed;
- Helps balance out the energetic fields at the end of Reiki attunements or sessions;
- It is quite helpful in "softening" the 21 days healing crisis after the Reiki attunements;

Harmony has the following uses:

- When printed and displayed in a room, the symbol attracts energies and entities of harmony. Consequently, any activity in that room will resonate with this symbol's harmonious vibration. When combined with Hosanna, these symbols create a deeply peaceful and harmonious atmosphere;
- Use Harmony + Cho Ku Rei + Sei He Ki in the Reiki self-treatment to relax and create a peaceful environment;
- After a Reiki attunement or treatment on others, you can apply this symbol on the patient to assist them in their transition toward a heightened vibrational state;

- During the 21 days of self-healing that follow the Reiki attunement, some practitioners may experience various symptoms like yawning, fatigue, or even dizziness, insomnia, and nausea. Meditating with this symbol and incorporating it into your self-treatment can mitigate many of these symptoms;

THE FLOWER OF LIFE

While the "Flower of Life" is introduced in the Shamballa Reiki system, it's recognized across various cultures and spiritual practices. Its shape is derived from Sacred Geometry and is believed to predate even ancient Egypt.

The Flower of Life has 3 main attributes:

- It emanates a high vibration that can gradually help you grow from a spiritual standpoint;
- Brings the energy of unity and interconnection and promotes the concept of "everything is one";
- Plays a crucial role in sealing and enhancing the attunement effects of Shamballa Reiki;

The Flower of Life has the following uses:

- Simply visualizing or printing this symbol allows one to harness its high-vibrational energy;
- Meditating on this symbol reveals its profound meaning: our interconnectedness and existence beyond the material realm;
- The Flower of Life is believed to hold the keys to life's blueprint, spiritual evolution, and the mysteries of the Universe;

The Flower of Life is deeply embedded in the tapestry of history and spirituality. Engaging with this symbol is like tapping into ancestral wisdom. Many people find solace in its patterns, seeing in its interlocking circles a reflection of life's cyclical nature, the ebb and flow of experiences, and the profound interconnectedness of all beings.

While its geometrical precision appeals to the logical mind, its spiritual essence touches the soul.

MERKABA STAR

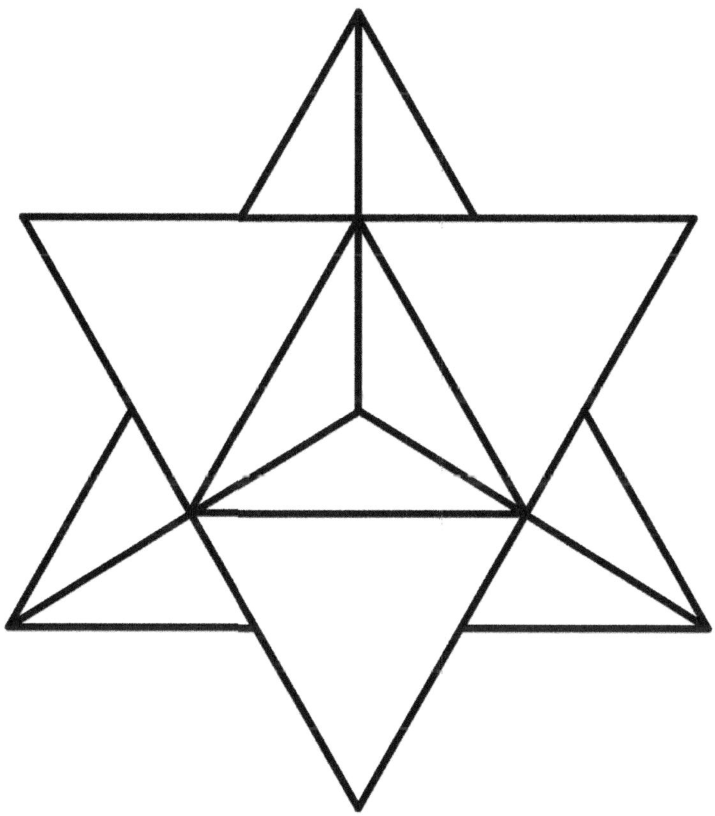

This is another example of Sacred Geometry, which apparently has its origins in Jewish esoteric thought.
Some academics think that this sign traces back to the existence of the mythical continent of Atlantis. The Merkaba Star is also incorporated into the Shamballa Reiki system.

Merkaba Star has 3 main attributes:

- Offers significant protection once you integrate it into your energetic system;
- Plays a crucial role in your spiritual development by unlocking higher states of consciousness;
- Enables the inner self to harmoniously connect to the higher self, leading to an optimum self-awareness;

Merkaba Star has the following uses:

- Visualize your physical and energetic bodies within the Merkaba Star when meditating to create a divine shield. Keep in mind that this can potentially affect the degree to which you are able to interact with others;
- Activate inert spiritual qualities. The more you work with this potent, energetic structure, the more inclined you will be to raise your awareness and consciousness;

- One of the effects of working with the elements of Sacred Geometry, including the Merkaba Star, is the activation of the Soul Star, crown, third eye, and heart chakras;
- To understand the true nature of spirituality, an inner self-ascension has to take place. The Merkaba Star can gradually enhance the connection between the inner self and the higher self;

METATRON'S CUBE

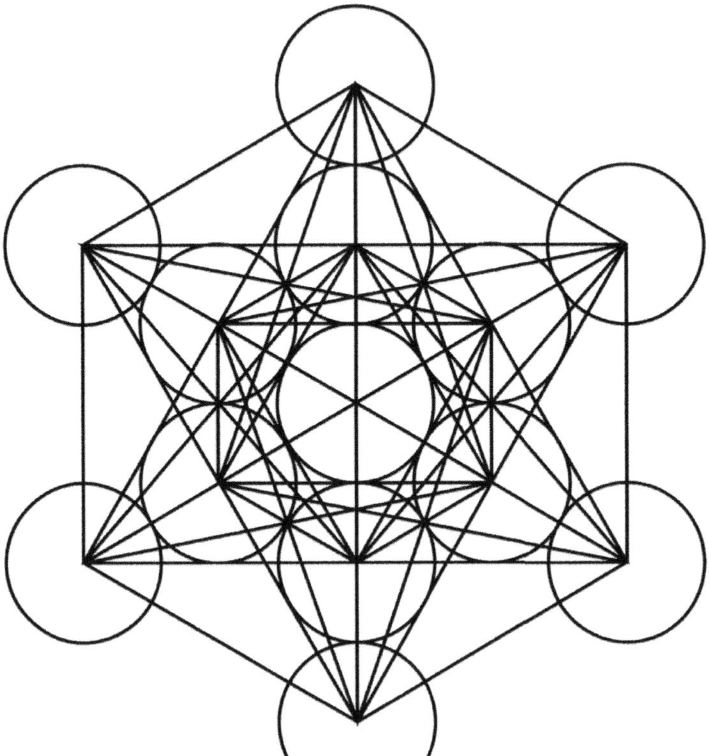

Metatron's Cube encompasses all the geometric shapes known to exist in the Universe. You can access this complex spiritual structure through Shamballa Reiki for energetic protection and spiritual growth. It's similar to Merkaba Star, which operates in perfect harmony with.

Metatron's Cube has 3 main attributes:

- Provides energetic protection while offering the potential for spiritual ascension;
- Its constant use helps raise your consciousness and awareness;
- Brings balance and harmony wherever you place it;

Metatron's Cube has the following uses:

- Similar to Merkaba Star, Metatron's Cube is one of the most potent forms of energetic protection. Visualize the structure surrounding your physical body during meditation. It's best to consider a quick, energetic cleansing method before engaging with Metatron's Cube to prevent any negative energies and intentions affecting you;

- During meditation or self-treatment, you can invoke the Merkaba Star first and then the Metatron's Cube to receive the optimum version for your current vibration level. If you stay connected to their energy for a prolonged period, your whole energetic structure will gradually change;

- Metatron's Cube acts like a cosmic vessel. This structure can help transport your energetic body to other worlds in meditation. From there on, you may receive access to new spiritual knowledge. Ask your Reiki guides for support. Always keep the Cube around you as it will filter out residual and unnecessary energies;

- This energetic structure also has a cleansing and activation effect over your primary and trans-personal chakras (outside the physical body). These offer the potential of accessing new stages of consciousness;

- Constantly working with Archangel Metatron's energy will allow you to channel fresh insights from the higher planes of existence;

LEN SO MY

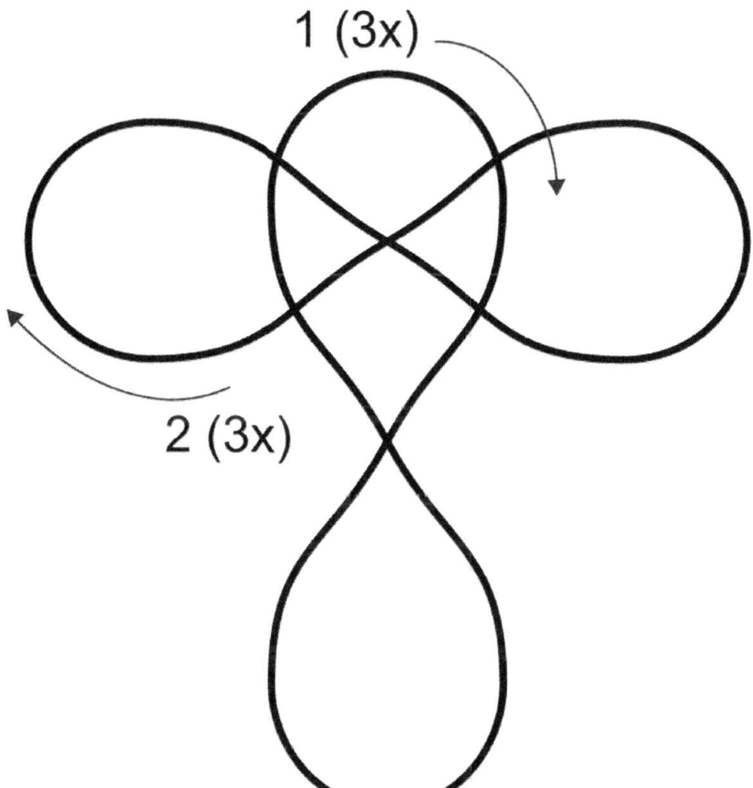

While not tied to a particular Reiki system, this symbol melds the infinite symbol from Sekhem Reiki with the angelic realm's essence of pure, unconditional love.

Len So My has the following attributes:

- Len So My holds the power to dispel sentiments of abandonment, loss, indifference, or unworthiness.
- It serves as a potent remedy to release the guilt associated with past mistakes;
- It's a representation of pure, unconditional love, a vibrational frequency that resonates with the highest intentions of healing, compassion, and self-acceptance;
- It washes over your emotional layers, nurturing feelings of solace, affection, forgiveness, and empathy for both yourself and others;

Len So My has the following uses:

- Incorporating Len So My into your Reiki self-treatment routine can be an enriching experience. To do this, activate the symbol by drawing or visualizing it on your palms and then focusing on the crown chakra, the energy center that connects to our universal consciousness. Visualize the symbol's energy flowing through your body, enveloping you in its warm, nurturing embrace. Feel the energy surrounding you aligning with your own vibrational frequency;

- Alternatively, you can activate the vertical component along the entire length of your body, encompassing both front and back, with the loops intersecting around the Solar Plexus region. The horizontal infinity segment can be traced in the area of your head, with the loops converging at the third eye chakra.

Len So My is more than a simple tool but a profound spiritual guide that can lead you to greater self-awareness, love, and harmony within your life.

OM BENZA SATTO HUNG

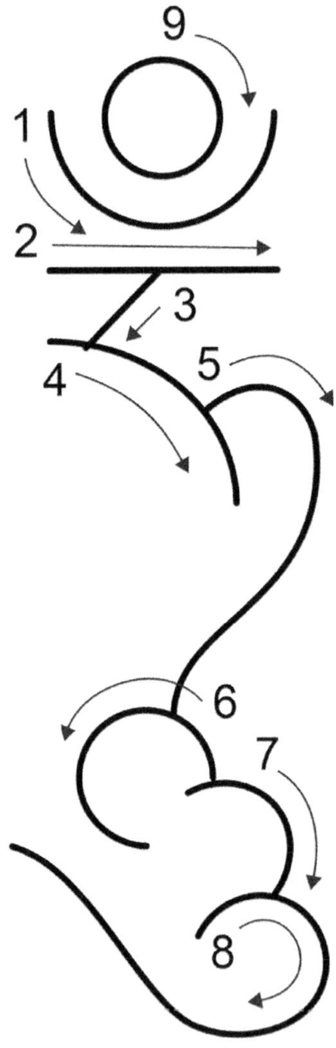

Om Benza Satto Hung is more than a mantra but a powerful sound embodiment with purification at its core. This ancient and resonant chant harmonizes the energy fields, clearing residual and negative energies that may be lingering in your aura or space.

When you tap into its high vibration, you're engaging with a frequency that transcends ordinary consciousness, aligning with a state of clarity, peace, and spiritual elevation. Its transformative power reaches the depths of the soul, cleansing and revitalizing on a profound level.

As a mantra, Om Benza Satto Hung's full potential can be unlocked through mindful practice. Reciting its name while meditating on its meaning creates a synergistic effect, enhancing both the auditory and intuitive senses. The combination of sound, vibration, and intention resonates within, awakening inner wisdom and a deeper connection to universal truth.

The crown chakra is associated with divine wisdom and understanding. Activate Om Benza Satto Hung above this energy center to pave the way for spiritual enlightenment and higher consciousness. Whether for self-treatment or meditation, positioning the mantra here bridges the physical and spiritual realms, facilitating a flow of energy that nourishes the whole being.

Utilizing Om Benza Satto Hung in your practice isn't merely a method but a profound spiritual journey. Its vibration reaches beyond the surface, guiding you to inner purity, liberation from limiting beliefs, and a deeper connection with the universal energy that permeates all existence. Whether you're a practitioner, a healer, or someone seeking personal growth, embracing this mantra can transform your spiritual development.

CELLULAR HEALING

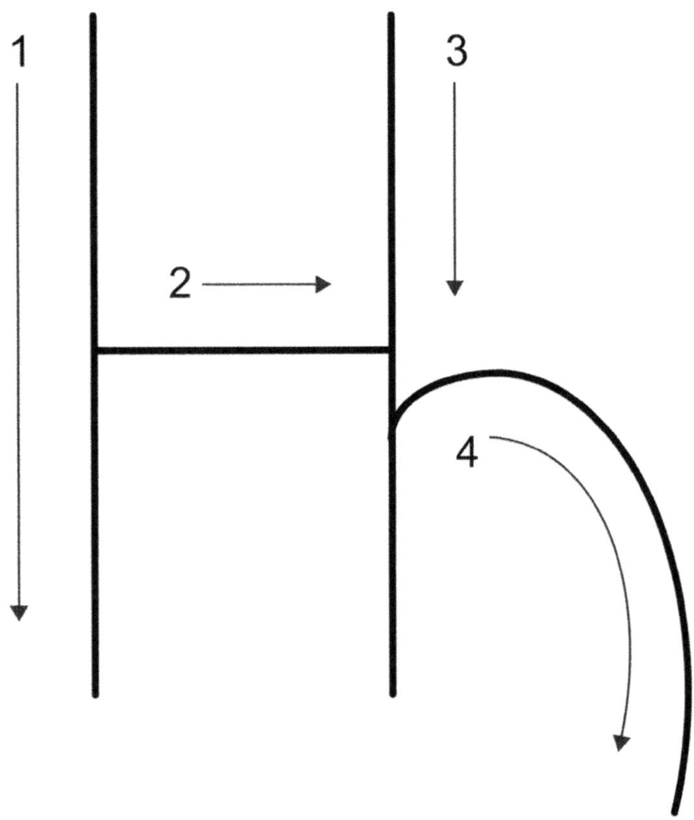

The Cellular Healing symbol is a profound and specialized tool in energy healing that doesn't belong to any particular Reiki system. It was channeled by the renowned master Kathleen Coree.

Cellular Healing has one main attribute:

- It addresses past sufferings and traumas, which aren't merely stored as memories or emotional residues but as energy imprints that can impact holistic well-being. This symbol helps to access and release these energies, transforming them into a state of healing and growth;

Cellular Healing has the following uses:

- Within self-treatment, use Cellular Healing + Zonar to target the negative energy imprinted by past traumas and restore balance within the soul's journey;
- It acts as a catalyst for transmuting past energy into light and supports healing at the cellular level;
- By addressing the underlying energetic patterns of past traumas, it may prevent potential imbalances within the physical body;

The Cellular Healing is a holistic approach to healing that recognizes the interconnectedness of our physical, emotional, and spiritual selves. Its utilization in Reiki or other energy healing practices can create opportunities for profound transformation and growth.

For those seeking to heal past wounds and rejuvenate their spirit, the Cellular Healing symbol stands as a powerful ally. Use it in self-treatment or integrate it into professional healing sessions as a gentle guide towards wholeness and inner peace.

HEAL THE HEALERS

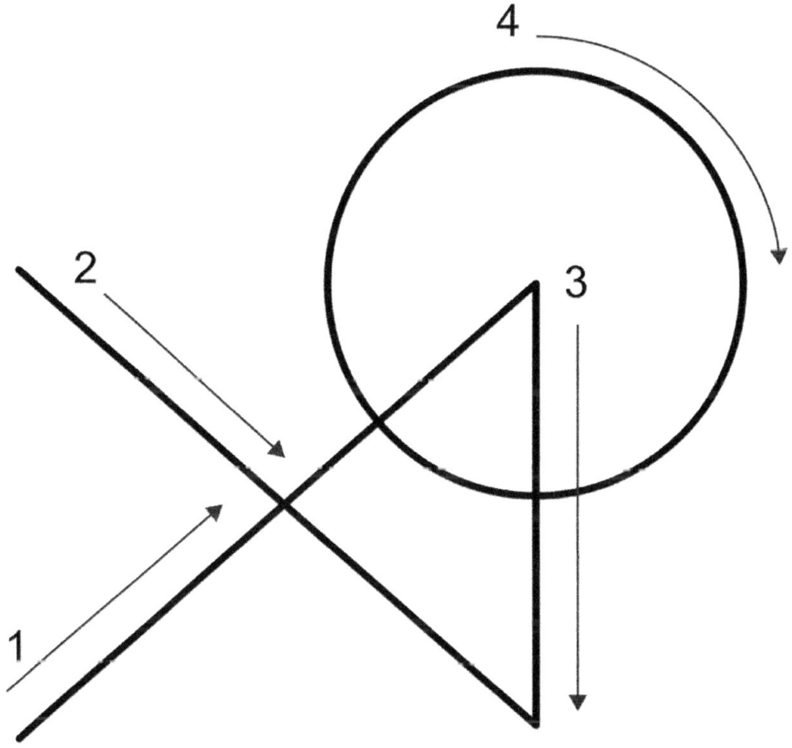

The Heal The Healers symbol, often linked to the Shamballa Reiki system, was introduced by Loril Moondream.

Heal The Healers has one primary attribute:

- Assist those who are using healing techniques to help others;

Heal The Healers has the following uses:

- The symbol's physical presence or energetic activation aids in removing negative and leftover energies from your chakras and energy fields;
- You can include this symbol in your self-treatment routine or visualize it in front of you during meditation. In just a few minutes, its vibrations will start to cleanse your energy structures;
- Add Cho Ku Rei to enhance its positive effect;
- This symbol is linked with the unconditional love extended by Kwan Yin, the Buddhist embodiment of female divinity, representing compassion, understanding, and love;
- Heal The Healers symbol resonates with the crown and heart chakras. Therefore, you can activate it on these two energy centers before starting your Reiki self-treatment;

HIGH LOW GOD SELVES

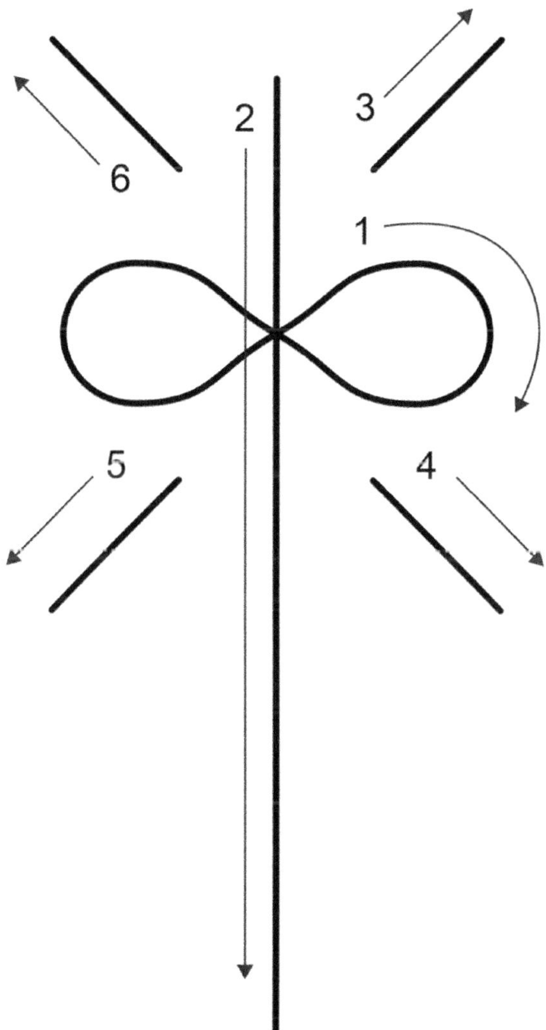

The High Low God Selves symbol belongs to the Seichim Reiki system.

High Low God Selves has 3 main attributes:

- Helps you connect to the Light of Christ, which is a powerful manifestation of the universal life force energy;
- Helps your inner self connect to your higher self, thus enhancing the potential for spiritual awakening;
- Brings together the energy of compassion, wisdom, and understanding;

High Low God Selves has the following uses:

- You can activate it either above the crown chakra before self-treatment or visualize it in meditation in front of you;
- The High Low God Selves will open the gateway toward its pure energy, engulfing you within it;

ANGEL WINGS

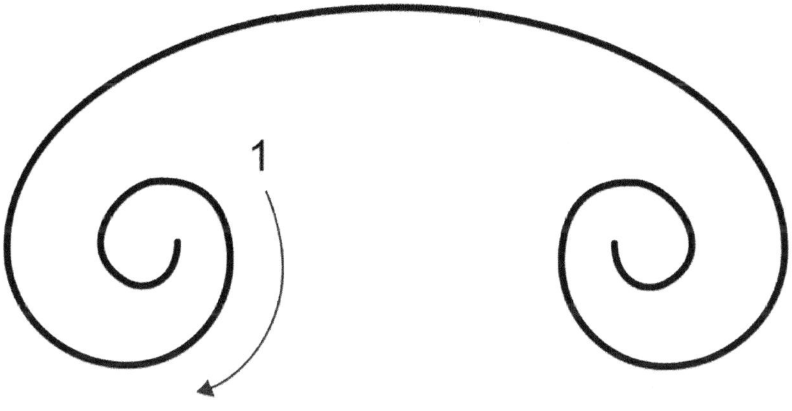

While the Angel Wings symbol is part of the Seichim Reiki system, it's also recognized in various other spiritual practices.

Angel Wings has 3 main attributes:

- Similar to the High Low God Selves, it helps the inner self connect to the higher self;
- It taps into the healing energies of angels, Reiki spirit guides, and divine entities, aiding in the channeling of insights from this realm;
- It can also balance the energy of the two brain hemispheres;

Angel Wings has the following uses:

- Activate it on the Soul Star chakra to enhance the universal life force energy flow;
- When activated together with Sei He Ki on the crown chakra, it will balance the energy of the two brain hemispheres. This leads to an increased capacity for learning and the potential for manifesting divine wisdom;
- You can also activate both Angel Wings and Gnosa on the crown chakra to increase cerebral activity and become more open to learning;

- Within meditation or when activated on the crown chakra prior to the Reiki self-treatment, the Angel Wings symbol will help improve your connection with your guardian angel, Reiki spirit guides, and divine entities;

- With constant use, this symbol will facilitate the connection between your inner self and higher self. In turn, this will enable a spiritual awakening that can manifest differently for each and every person;

MALE-FEMALE SYMBOL

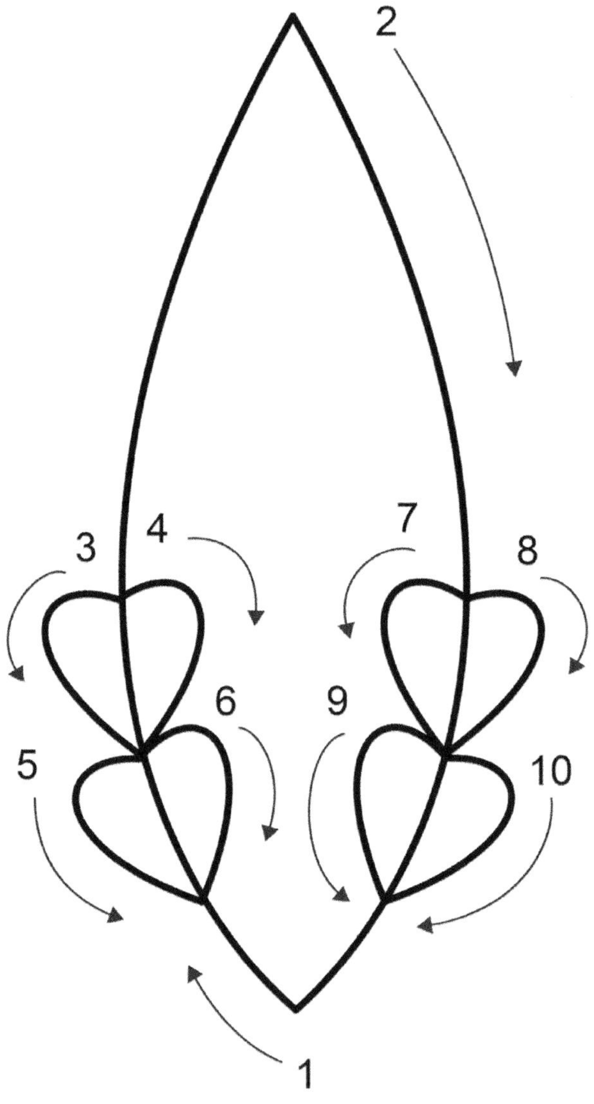

Moving on to the rich tapestry of symbols within the Seichim Reiki system, we arrive at a particularly fascinating and essential symbol known as the Male-Female Symbol, which serves as an energetic bridge, embodying a fundamental principle of universal duality.

Male-Female symbol has the following attributes:

- The symbol has a transformative ability to harmonize an individual's male and female energies. These energies represent the dualistic nature of all existence, encompassing attributes such as strength and compassion, logic and intuition, action and receptivity.
- By creating a balance, this symbol aids in aligning the individual with a state of inner wholeness, paving the way for personal growth and self-realization;
- It enhances communication across diverse gender identities, serving as a channel for empathy and mutual understanding;

Male-Female symbol has the following uses:

- Activate it during meditation or self-treatment to access its balancing energy;
- Visualize it between yourself and another individual as a connecting link that fosters mutual understanding;

THIRD-EYE MEMORY

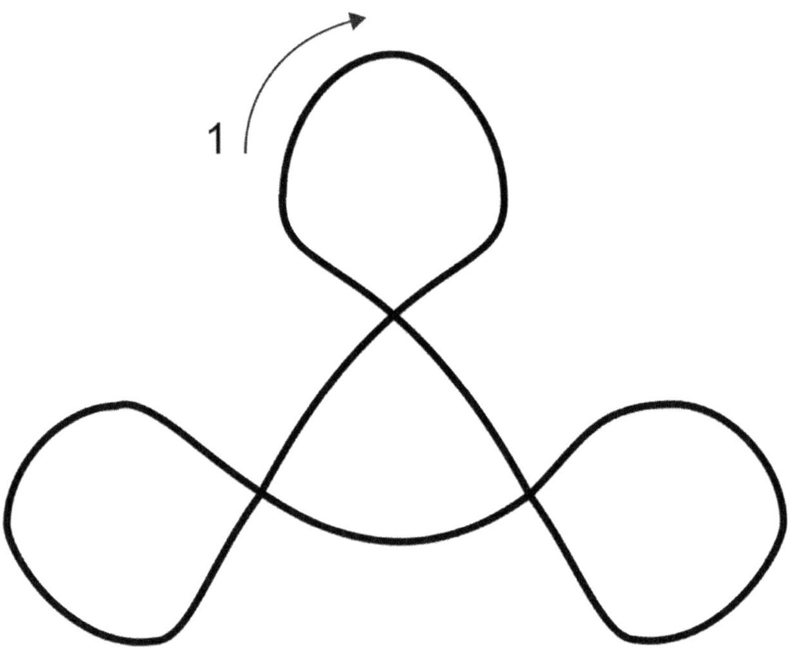

Reiki Master Derek O'Sullivan channeled the Third-Eye Memory symbol, which isn't exclusive to any specific system.

Third-Eye Memory has one main attribute:

- Its primary function is to facilitate the recall of insights that you might have encountered during meditations or spiritual practices. Whether these are fleeting impressions or subtle intuitions, the symbol acts as a bridge to the subconscious mind, enabling you to access and integrate these experiences into your conscious awareness;

Third-Eye Memory has the following uses:

- To harness the power of this symbol, you can activate it before any meditation by focusing on the third-eye chakra. This chakra, located in the forehead between the eyebrows, is the center of intuition, insight, and spiritual vision. By aligning the Third-Eye Memory symbol with this energy center, you create a synergy that enhances your ability to tap into and retrieve the wisdom stored within;

The Third-Eye Memory represents a gateway to the deeper layers of the self, bridging the gap between the seen and unseen, the known and unknown. Use it as a practical tool and a mystical pathway to gain tangible insights toward the intangible realms of spirit and consciousness.

THE MYSTIC KNOT

Though rooted in the ancient wisdom of Feng-Shui, the Mystic Knot transcends mere symbolism to encapsulate a profound philosophical concept. It's a visual and spiritual metaphor that weaves together multiple layers of meaning, resonating with universal truths that are both timeless and deeply relevant.

The Mystic Knot is often seen as a symbol of the unbroken lineage and continuity of Buddha's teachings, embodying the eternal wisdom that flows through time and space, never beginning and never ending.

It also represents the endless cycle of our spirit's manifestation within multiple planes of existence. This is reflective of the belief in reincarnation and the interplay of karma, where our actions and experiences continue to weave the fabric of our existence across lifetimes.

With its never-ending loops, the Mystic Knot symbolizes infinite wisdom and compassion. It speaks of the boundless nature of proper understanding, love, and the persistence of life through the ages. Its elegant complexity conveys teachings that are at once simple and profound, guiding us toward deeper personal knowledge in relation to the universe.

Mystic Knot has the following uses:

- Keep a representation next to you for an easier connection with its energy;
- Meditate on the symbol to deepen your relationship to its underlying principles, fostering a sense of unity and infinite potential;

RA TA RIO

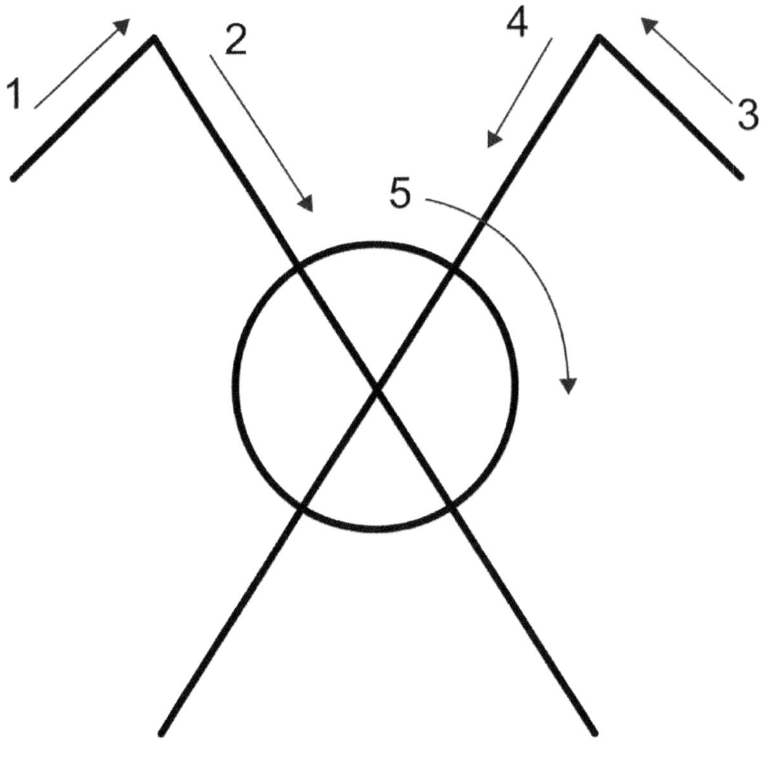

The Ra Ta Rio symbol is not tied to any specific Reiki system. Instead, it emerged from the intuitive and spiritual insights of Christopher Penczak, a renowned spiritual practitioner and Reiki Master.

Ra Ta Rio has the following main attribute:

- This symbol represents a unique aspect of spiritual exploration and healing. It helps harmonize the link between the inner self and the conscious mind by creating peace and acceptance with one's shadow self;

The shadow self is the part of us that holds repressed feelings, fears, desires, and past traumas. While these aspects are often hidden, they have a profound influence on our behavior and, of course, overall well-being. Ra Ta Rio acts as a bridge, encouraging an honest engagement with these hidden parts of ourselves.

Healing goes beyond symptoms and into a journey of wholeness and acceptance. The symbol has the potential to support our efforts in recognizing and transforming the shadow aspects of ourselves, leading to more authentic healing.

Ra Ta Rio has the following uses:

- Integrate it in meditations and self-treatment to encourage yourself to look within. Become fearless in front of unsettling aspects and even embrace the opportunity to "confront" them;

- Learn to foster self-acceptance and carve a path toward genuine equilibrium;

Ra Ta Rio is a spiritual ally for those seeking to journey within and make peace with all aspects of themselves. It can guide us towards a deeper connection with ourselves, unlocking the door to authenticity and fulfillment.

ANTI-BACTERIAL

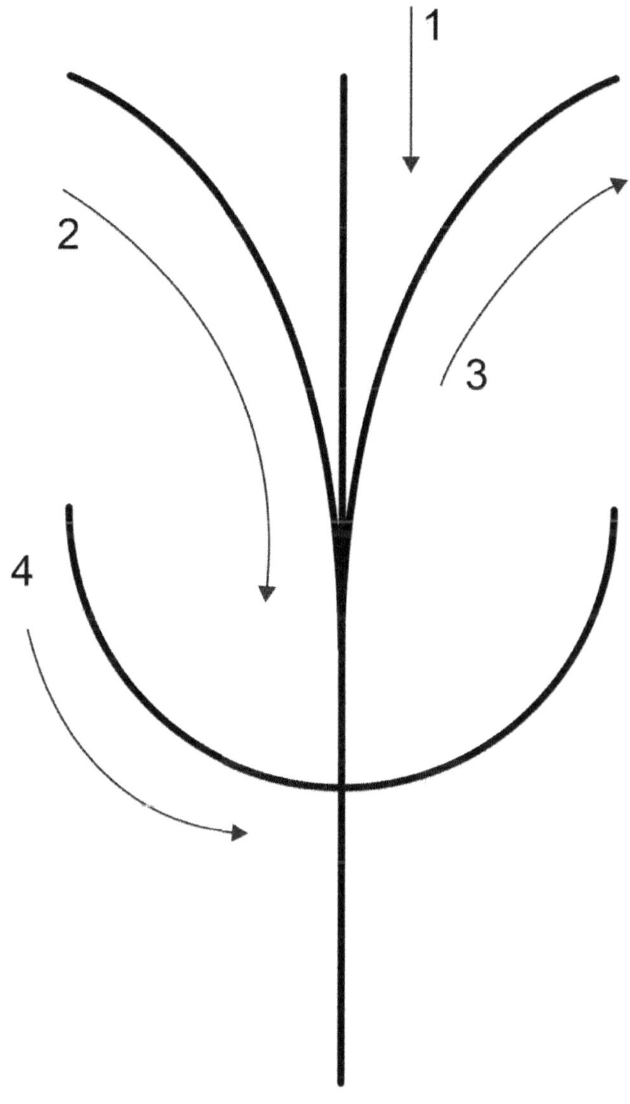

The Anti-Bacterial symbol, a profound and specialized tool, was channeled by spiritual practitioner and Reiki Master Christopher Penczak. While traditional Reiki symbols target general healing and balance, the Anti-Bacterial symbol zeroes in on specific therapeutic areas, paving the way for specialized healing and restoration. Its applications are both pragmatic and deeply spiritual, merging the physical and energetic realms.

Anti-Bacterial has the following attributes:

- The Anti-Bacterial symbol primarily aids in eliminating bacteria causing infections. It stimulates the energetic level to help flush out the toxins, thus speeding up the healing process;

- The symbol has a unique ability to work on the vital field of pathogenic bacteria or parasites, disintegrating them. This aspect moves beyond conventional healing, targeting the energy dynamics of diseases and disorders;

- The Anti-Bacterial symbol also extends its healing scope to removing seasonal allergies. Working on subtle energy levels addresses the root causes and symptoms of allergies, creating a more harmonious state within the organism;

Anti-Bacterial has the following uses:

- To target the infection's energy print directly, activate 3 x Cho Ku Rei + 3 x Anti-Bacterial + 3 x Cho Ku Rei above the affected area. Do this daily until you eliminate the problem. Consider adding 3 x Motor Zanon for an enhanced effect;

The Anti-Bacterial symbol represents a highly targeted and potent healing tool within the spiritual practitioner's arsenal. It bridges the gap between physical ailments and energetic imbalances, offering immediate and profound solutions.

For infections, allergies, or other bacterial issues, this symbol offers an alternative healing route, surpassing traditional limits and delving deeper into understanding and healing.

ANTI-DEPRESSION

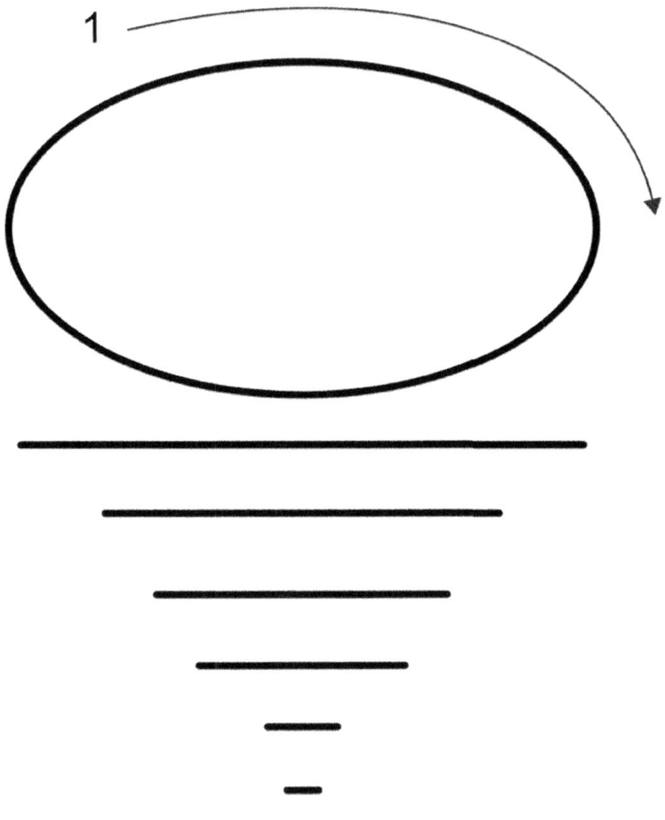

The Anti-Depression symbol is a specific tool within the Violet Flame Reiki system.

Anti-Depression has the following attribute:

- While many factors can contribute to depression, biochemical imbalances within the body often play a significant role. The Anti-Depression symbol aims to boost the production of endorphins, the body's natural "feel-good" chemicals, and balance the levels of serotonin, a key neurotransmitter linked to mood. By working on these biochemical aspects, the symbol provides a holistic approach to alleviating depression;

Anti-Depression has the following uses:

- Apply the symbol directly on the third-eye chakra and its back projection to gradually remove the negative energy of depression. Stay in this position for about 10 minutes;

- Activate it on food and beverages before consuming them. As mentioned, this will help stimulate the production of endorphins in the body and help lower the symptoms associated with depression;

The Anti-Depression symbol provides a pathway to healing that transcends traditional medical approaches, addressing depression's multifaceted nature.

IMPORTANT: *It is essential to recognize that while the Anti-Depression symbol offers valuable support in managing depression, it is not a replacement for professional medical treatment when needed. Working with a mental health professional, in conjunction with spiritual and energy healing practices, often provides the most balanced and effective approach to dealing with depression. The Anti-Depression symbol then becomes part of a broader healing strategy, offering a spiritual dimension to recovery and well-being.*

OM MANI PADME HUM

ཨོཾམཎིཔདྨེཧཱུྃ

"Om Mani Padme Hum" is a complex and profound series of concepts that together form one of spiritual traditions' most revered and influential mantras. Often associated with Tibetan Buddhist practices, this mantra encompasses an intricate philosophy and an array of profound meanings. Its multifaceted meaning offers a gateway into deeper understanding and connection with the self and the cosmos.

Translation and Meaning:

The mantra "Om Mani Padme Hum" can be roughly translated as:

"An impure body becomes pure through the speech and mind of Buddha - through compassion and altruistic intentions, like a lotus, aspires to become an indivisible unity through divine values."

- **Om:** Represents the essence of enlightenment and the unity of body, speech, and mind;

- **Mani:** Refers to the "jewel" of compassion, altruism, and love;

- **Padme:** Symbolizes the "lotus," a representation of wisdom, purity, and spiritual awakening;

- **Hum:** Denotes indivisibility and the realization of divine values;

Uses and Benefits:

- Chant or listen to the mantra during meditations, Reiki self-treatment, or other spiritual practices to align with your higher consciousness, compassion, and inner peace;

- When played continuously in a room, the mantra's vibrations can have a cleansing, purifying effect, raising the overall vibrational frequency. This creates an ambiance of tranquility, spiritual connection, and positive energy flow;

It's important to acknowledge that not everyone resonates with this vibration level. Individual experiences with this mantra can vary widely, reflecting personal spiritual paths and inner states.

OM GAYATRI

The Gayatri Mantra, an ancient and revered chant, embodies a declaration of appreciation and healing. Dating back to approximately 3000 BC, it holds a special place in the Vedic tradition, often referred to as the "Mother of the Vedas" - the foundational spiritual texts of ancient Indian culture.

Meaning and Significance:

The Gayatri Mantra is a universal prayer that seeks spiritual awakening and enlightenment. Its specific words invoke the divine light of the Supreme Being to illuminate our intellect, guide our thoughts, and lead us down a path of wisdom and understanding.

Gayatri Mantra has the following attributes:

- Chanting or listening to the Gayatri Mantra brings balance and stability to the mind and soul;
- It can effectively remove negative energies and emotions such as stress, fear, and anxiety, helping to create a state of inner peace and clarity;
- The mantra is known to detoxify the body by cleansing it of harmful toxins and impurities;
- Its vibration resonates with the body's energy centers, enhancing overall wellness and vitality;

An ancient saying about the Gayatri Mantra suggests: *"...if a person goes into the Gayatri deep meditation once a week for a total of 9 weeks, that person doesn't get sick for the rest of their life."*

Though this statement may be understood symbolically rather than literally, it emphasizes the mantra's profound potential for healing and transformation.

Gayatri Mantra has the following uses:

- Incorporate Gayatri Mantra into daily spiritual practices, meditations, or therapeutic sessions;
- You can chant it aloud, silently recite it within the mind, or listen to it as part of a meditative practice;
- The proper pronunciation and respectful approach to the mantra are essential to unlock its full potential and benefits;

Cultural and Spiritual Legacy:

The Gayatri Mantra remains a unique spiritual tool that transcends cultural boundaries, offering timeless wisdom for those seeking personal growth and connection.

However, please note that while the Gayatri Mantra is indeed powerful and therapeutic, it is best used in conjunction with other wellness practices and should not be considered a substitute for professional medical care.

AT MATA

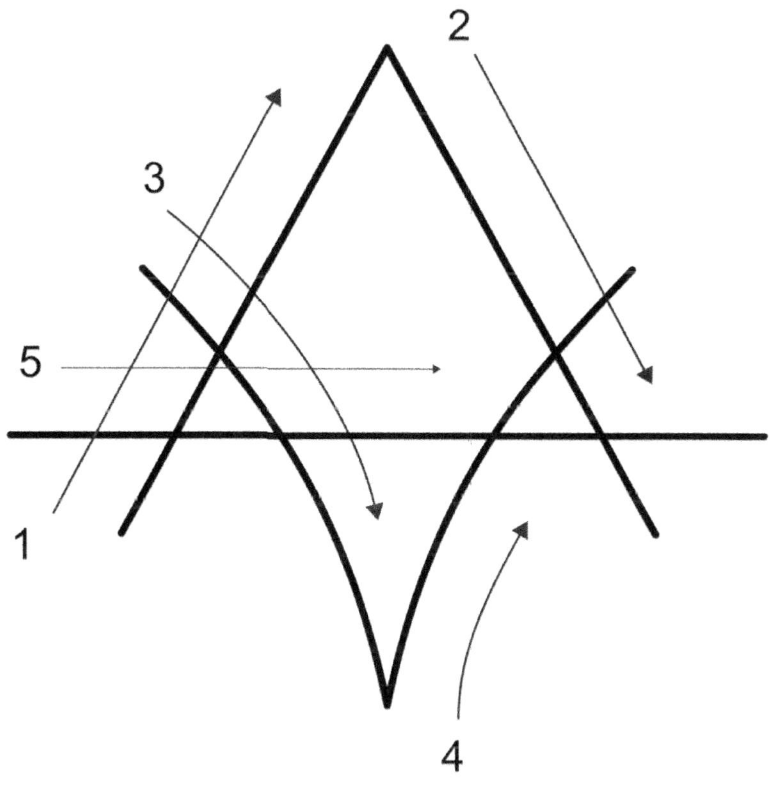

At Mata is a unique spiritual concept that doesn't belong to any specific Reiki system. It serves as a spiritual tool and emblem, embodying profound ideas about the interconnectedness of mind, body, and spirit.

At Mata has the following attributes:

- It represents a guidepost for comprehending the essential connection between spiritual and emotional healing. It emphasizes that one must address the mental and emotional dimensions to achieve optimal physical well-being;
- It helps align your consciousness with the realization that mental and emotional healing is vital for overall wellness;
- At Mata serves as a spiritual gateway that leads you toward inner balance, self-realization, and spiritual awakening;
- As a guiding light for your inner journey, it can inspire reflection, mindfulness, and a more profound connection with your true self;

At Mata has the following uses:

- Its mere presence or contemplation can facilitate the removal of mental blockages and obstacles that may hinder personal growth and self-awareness;

- You can actively engage with At Mata by visualizing it during meditations, allowing its energy to resonate within you and guide your thoughts and emotions;

At Mata acts as an enduring philosophy that recognizes the complex interplay between the physical, mental, and emotional aspects of our being. Its wisdom transcends conventional boundaries, offering guidance and healing to those who seek a harmonious and holistic approach to life.

LIVE LI

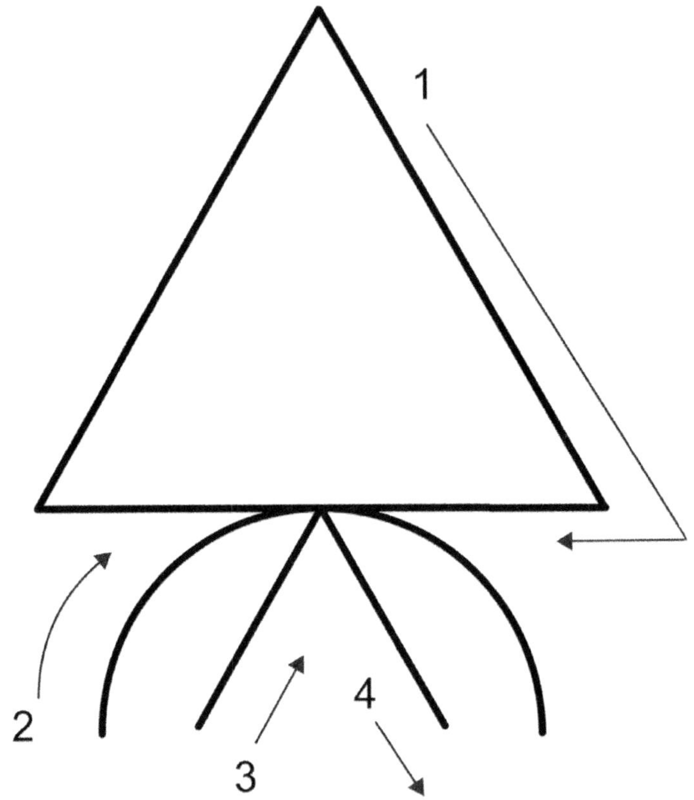

Live Li belongs to no particular Reiki system. It serves as an energetic tool with specialized applications in cleansing and purification, mainly focusing on removing negative energy prints associated with bacteria, viruses, and infections.

Live Li has the following main attribute:

- Eradicates the energetic imprints of harmful microorganisms such as bacteria and viruses. This cleansing extends beyond the physical, affecting the subtle energy levels that influence overall well-being;

Live Li has the following uses:

- Activate or visualize it above your head as part of your preparation for meditations or self-treatment;
- Pronouncing its name three times amplifies its properties in the physical plane, allowing a deeper connection with the symbol and its healing power;
- Visualize Live Li forming into a tetrahedron, one of the basic geometric shapes often associated with spiritual energy;
- Guide this symbolic form through your entire body, with your intention leading its trajectory. As it moves, imagine it cleansing all residual and negative energies;

While similar to Motor Zanon, Live Li specifically focuses on dissolving the energy prints related to bacteria and infections. On the other hand, Motor Zanon can help eliminate various types of negative influences without the same specialized focus. By addressing both physical ailments (like infections) and energetic imbalances, Live Li encourages a holistic approach to healing and well-being.

Remember that you play an active role in the healing process due to the fact that you're consciously guiding the symbol toward the desired outcome.

KIR MALL

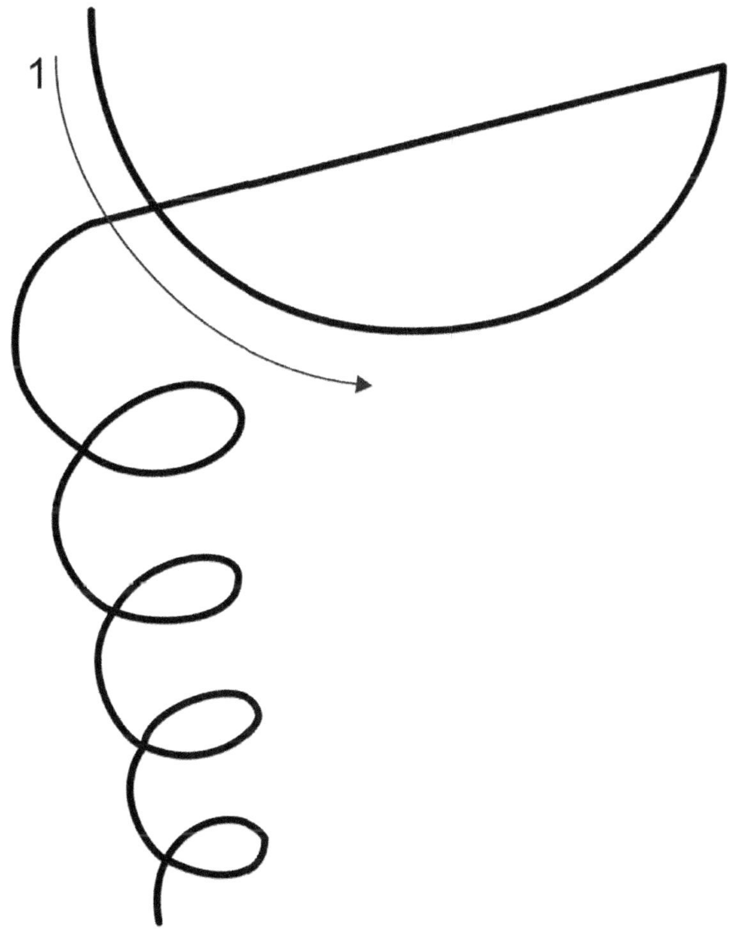

Kir Mall is not part of any traditional Reiki system. Reiki Master Christopher Penczak channeled it through his spiritual exploration. This symbol carries a particular resonance with the alleviation of physical fatigue and pain.

Kir Mall has the following attributes:

- It functions as a therapeutic tool to alleviate physical discomfort, fatigue, and various bodily pains;
- Its calming energy nourishes the subtle layers of one's being, promoting overall relaxation and well-being;
- The unique construction of Kir Mall includes four circles, each symbolizing one of the main primordial elements: fire (or heat), water, air, and earth. These elements are essential in various philosophical and healing traditions, representing different states and qualities of existence;
- By aligning with "Kir Mall," you encourage these elements to balance within your body, harmonizing their energies and fostering equilibrium;

Kir Mall has the following uses:

- You can use Kir Mall as a focal point in your meditation, visualizing it and allowing its energy to permeate your energetic body;

- Integrate it within your energy field to connect with the symbol's soothing and harmonizing properties, further enhancing your spiritual journey;

- Print Kir Mall and place it in your living or working space to allow its gentle, calming energy to surround you at all times. Its constant presence can foster a peaceful and balanced environment, supporting your daily activities and mental clarity;

Kir Mall provides a unique energetic gateway to soothe physical fatigue and pain while balancing the body's core elemental energies. Whether used in meditation, displayed in your surroundings, or integrated into other healing practices, it offers a nurturing and harmonizing influence that can enhance your overall well-being and spiritual alignment. Its gentle energy and symbolic depth make it a valuable asset for novice and experienced practitioners alike.

AUMINAHT

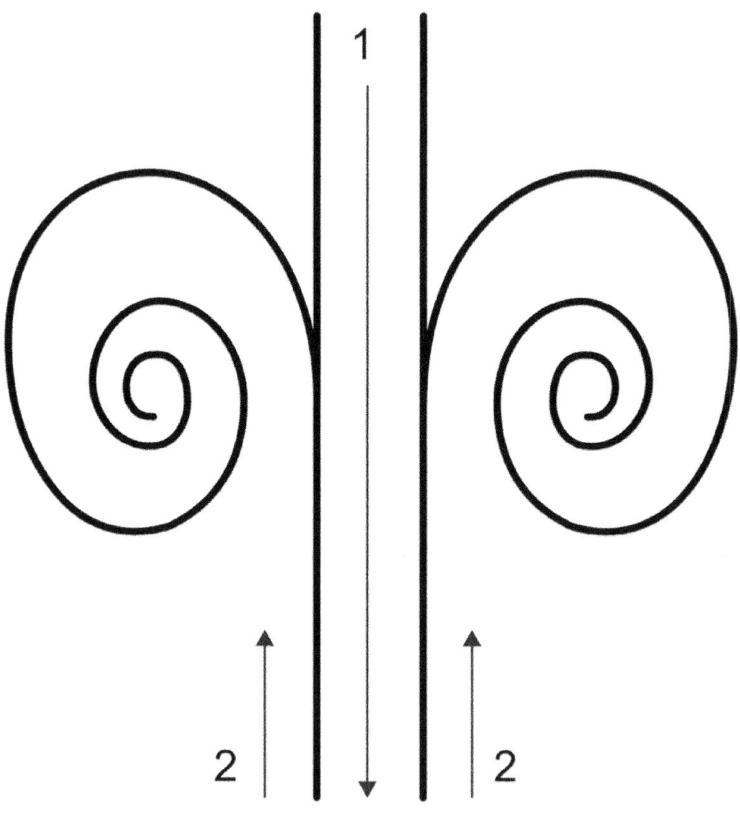

Auminaht is a profound spiritual symbol channeled by Reiki Master Jeff Johnson. Belonging to no particular Reiki system, it is predominantly applied to the back part of the body to profoundly influence the energy flow within the individual.

Auminaht has the following attributes:

- It serves as a potent tool in cleansing the meridians, the energetic pathways, and specifically the central channel known as Sushumna. This helps maintain a clear energy flow, ensuring an uninterrupted flow of universal energy;
- Apply Auminaht on the body's backside to assist in grounding, anchor the individual's energy to the Earth, and connect with earthly energies;
- Auminaht has a distinctive resonance with the Kundalini energy, aiding in its optimal rise, aligning this potent energy with the body's chakras, and harmonizing the physical and spiritual aspects of the being;

Auminaht has the following uses:

- By activating the symbol on the crown chakra and guiding it through your body, you help unite your mental energy with the heart chakra. This creates a beautiful synergy between rational thinking and emotional understanding, fostering a balanced and harmonious inner state;

- Activate Cho Ku Rei + Sei He Ki + Auminaht on the back of your body to cleanse the main energetic channel, Sushumna;

- Visualize Auminaht from the head to the toes to support deep grounding and open the minor chakras on your soles. This process releases residual energies, stimulates Kundalini's rise, balances the physical body, and opens your chakras to greater spiritual awareness;

- Apply it to the back of your body to ease muscle tension and back pain, promoting the free flow of universal and vital energy;

- Regular use of Auminaht before and after Reiki self-treatment progressively balances divine with telluric energies. This creates an emotional and spiritual equilibrium that's unique and deeply nurturing;

The Auminaht symbol invites a harmonious flow of energy that not only cleanses and grounds but also aligns and elevates your entire being.

DAZU

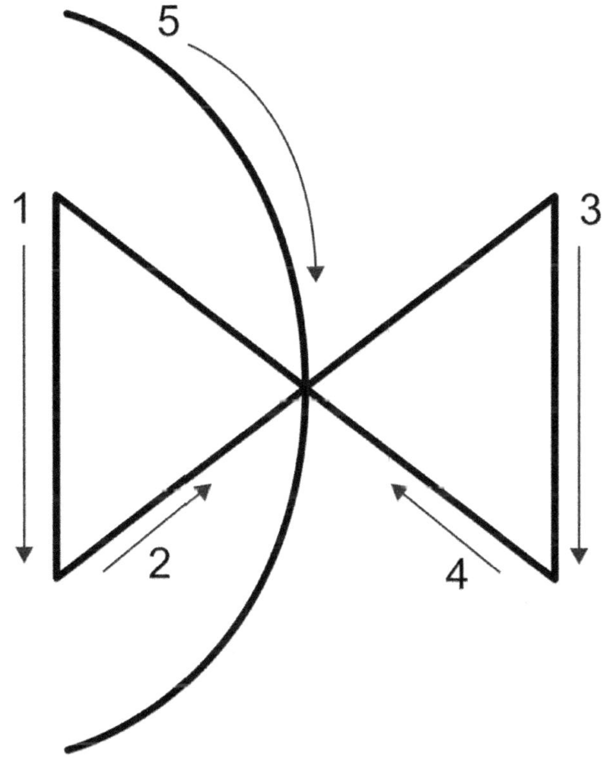

Dazu is not confined to any traditional Reiki system. Rather, it is a universal tool that connects individuals with nature's profound and nurturing energies. It serves as a conduit for healing, purification, and alignment with the natural world through its singular attribute and diverse applications.

Dazu has the following main attribute:

- The ability to act as a bridge between the individual and the beneficial energies found within nature;

Dazu has the following uses:

- Engaging with Dazu while outdoors allows you to filter and absorb nature's healing energies for physical and energetic balance, aligning you with the environment and enhancing your overall well-being;

- Activate Dazu on a plant to infuse it with a unique energy level that enables it to radiate healing vibrations all around. This process can potentially turn the plant into a living talisman, emanating nature's healing powers and enhancing the energy of your surroundings;

- It has a solid and immediate purifying effect on foods and beverages. By activating this symbol, you can cleanse them of toxins and negative energies, promoting quicker elimination from the body and contributing to overall health;

- You may use the symbol to activate and cleanse crystals, amulets, and other spiritual tools. By connecting them to nature's healing powers, Dazu purifies these objects of residual energies, enhancing their potency and aligning them with your healing intentions;

Dazu represents a versatile and accessible means of connecting with nature's abundant energies. Whether seeking physical detoxification, energetic alignment, or a deeper connection to the Earth, Dazu is the symbol you may want to consider. Its applications are as varied as nature itself, extending to plants, food, drinks, and spiritual tools.

By integrating Dazu into your daily practice, you can cultivate a more harmonious relationship with nature and yourself, grounding your existence in the wisdom and vitality of the natural world.

LUMA

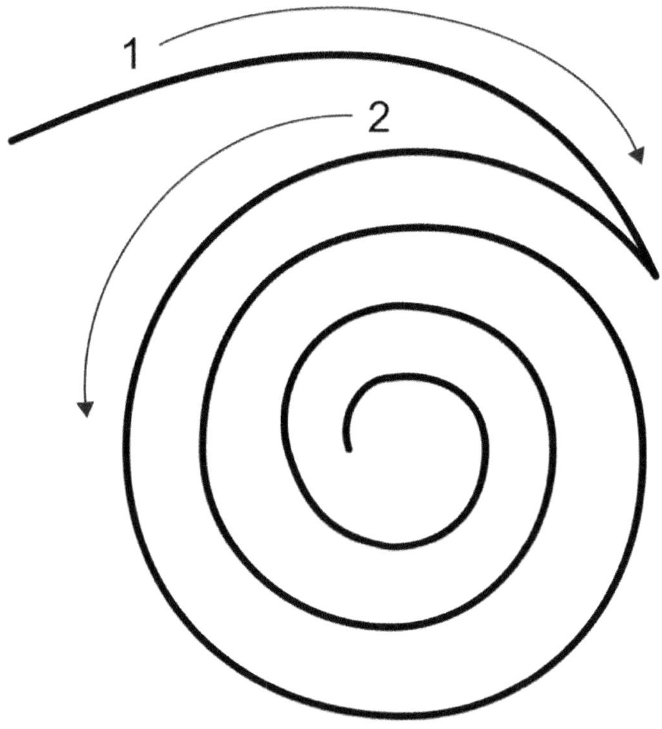

Luma is a unique symbol associated with the Shamballa Reiki Master level and was brought forth by Reiki Master Phyllis Brooks. It distinguishes itself through its resonance with feminine energy and its corresponding applications.

Luma has the following attributes:

- Luma is specifically attuned to the feminine aspects and is considered highly beneficial for women;
- It functions to harmonize the practitioner's personal feminine energy with the universal Yin, which represents the divine female energy present within the cosmos;
- By aligning these energies, Luma fosters emotional and energetic equilibrium between the individual and the surrounding environment, creating a serene and balanced state of being;

Luma has the following uses:

- You can use it to address and remedy imbalances, ailments, or issues localized in the female genital area, working to restore physical well-being and balance in this essential aspect of feminine health;
- Meditate on the symbol regularly to connect with its energy and gradually try to sense the balancing effects integrating within your structures;

- Display it in your favorite location to create an ongoing connection with its energetic imprint;
- Regularly engaging with its visual representation creates a continuous link to its healing and balancing properties, fostering a daily practice of alignment and well-being;

Luma represents a specialized tool within the Shamballa Reiki system, catering specifically to the needs and experiences of women. Its dual role in balancing feminine energy and healing physical imbalances in the female genital area makes it a uniquely empowering symbol for those drawn to its energy.

KUNDALINI BALANCE

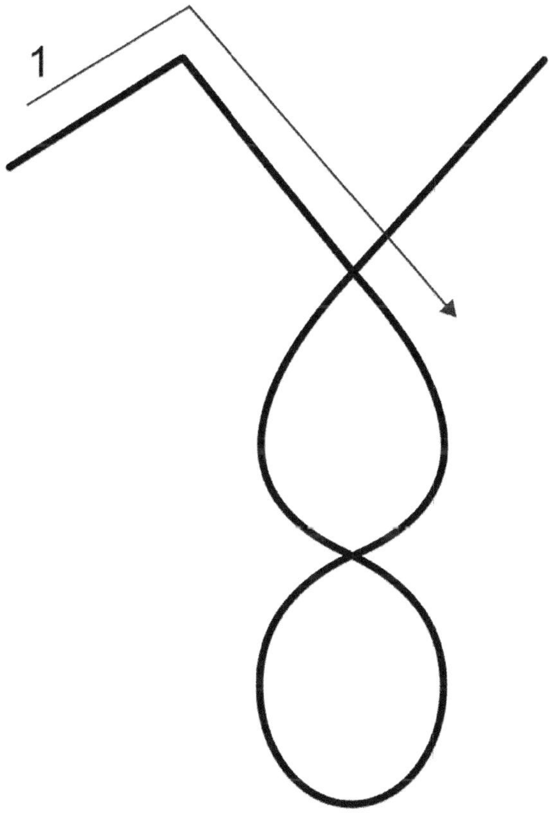

Kundalini Balance is another symbol channeled by Reiki Master Christopher Penczak. It is not affiliated with any specific Reiki system. The symbol serves as a spiritual tool for those seeking to explore and harmonize the Kundalini energy within themselves, opening doors to higher consciousness and spiritual exploration.

Kundalini Balance has the following attribute:

The primary function of this symbol is to aid in the gradual ascension of the Kundalini energy through the central energetic channel known as Sushumna for heightened self-awareness and unlocking new levels of consciousness;

NOTE: *The ascension of Kundalini energy is a delicate and potentially intense experience. Thus, it should be approached with care and at an individualized pace rather than force.*

Kundalini Balance has the following uses:

- Meditate on the symbol and visualize it as it integrates into your energetic structure;
- Rather than actively directing its movement, allow the symbol to unfold its "magic" naturally, guiding the energy as it awakens and rises;
- This visualization can help create a gentle and supportive environment for the Kundalini energy to ascend, balancing its movement through the Sushumna channel;

NYANSAPO

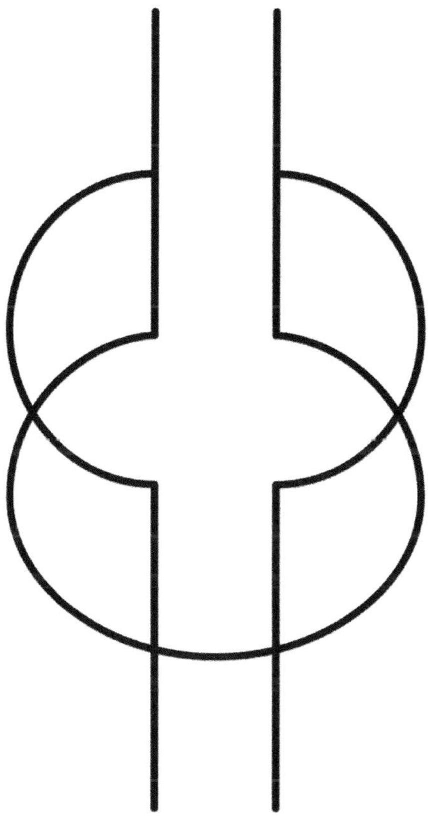

Nyansapo, also known as the "wisdom knot," is a traditional symbol from the Adinkra system, often found in West African culture. It represents a philosophical concept serving as a source of inspiration and reflection.

Nyansapo has the following attributes:

- It stands as a testament to intellectual pursuit and the accumulation of understanding through study and experience;
- It encourages continuous learning and growth, urging individuals to seek out new information and broaden their horizons;
- Nyansapo is also a celebration of wisdom, which encompasses the thoughtful application of knowledge, discernment, and good judgment;
- Connects intellect with intuition and ethical principles through wisdom;
- The intricate knot design of Nyansapo symbolizes the complexity of life's journey and the patience required to untangle its many challenges;
- It encourages perseverance, resilience, and the calm pursuit of one's goals, recognizing that wisdom and knowledge often come with time;

Nyansapo has the following uses:

- Visualize it during meditation, contemplating its interwoven design and what it represents in your personal journey;

- Print it out and place it in a space where you frequently see it so you can consistently expose yourself to its energetic imprint;

- Over time, this connection may spark a desire for self-improvement, intellectual curiosity, and the pursuit of wisdom in various aspects of life;

- Actively engage with it through journaling and self-reflection to align yourself with its values and find new avenues of growth;

Nyansapo encompasses intellectual and spiritual aspirations into one concept that connects to knowledge, wisdom, and patience. It serves as a guiding philosophy for those seeking to enrich their lives through learning and finding inspiration to approach life with a patient and thoughtful perspective.

OSRAM NE NSOROMMA

Osram Ne Nsoromma is a symbol of the Adinkra system, prevalent in West African culture, specifically among the Akan people of Ghana. It is often referred to as the "moon and star" symbol, encapsulating the spiritual and emotional connection between two people.

Attributes:

- **Love:** The symbol represents the pure, unconditional love that binds people together romantically and in friendship and familial relationships. It encourages empathy, compassion, and the selfless giving of oneself to others;

- **Affection:** Affection is portrayed as a natural extension of love, emphasizing warmth, tenderness, and a genuine fondness for others. It calls for genuine expression of feelings and emotional closeness;

- **Respect:** This is a key aspect of any healthy relationship, and it is embedded within the Osram Ne Nsoromma symbol. It implies mutual understanding, acceptance of differences, and the honoring of one another's individuality and dignity;

- **Understanding:** The symbol also highlights the importance of compassion, communication, and empathy in nurturing a fulfilling relationship. It promotes an open-hearted and open-minded approach to understanding others' feelings, thoughts, and behaviors;

Osram Ne Nsoromma has the following uses:

- Couples can simultaneously meditate on this symbol to strengthen their emotional bond and foster a deeper connection;

- Printing out the Osram Ne Nsoromma symbol and placing it in a shared living space can help fill the room with its positive energy;

- Individuals can reflect on the Osram Ne Nsoromma symbol to foster self-love and cultivate these attributes within other relationships;

Osram Ne Nsoromma is a beautiful representation of the core values that make relationships meaningful and fulfilling. Embodying love, affection, respect, and understanding offers guidance for those seeking to deepen their connections with others.

PERFECT LOVE AND TRUST

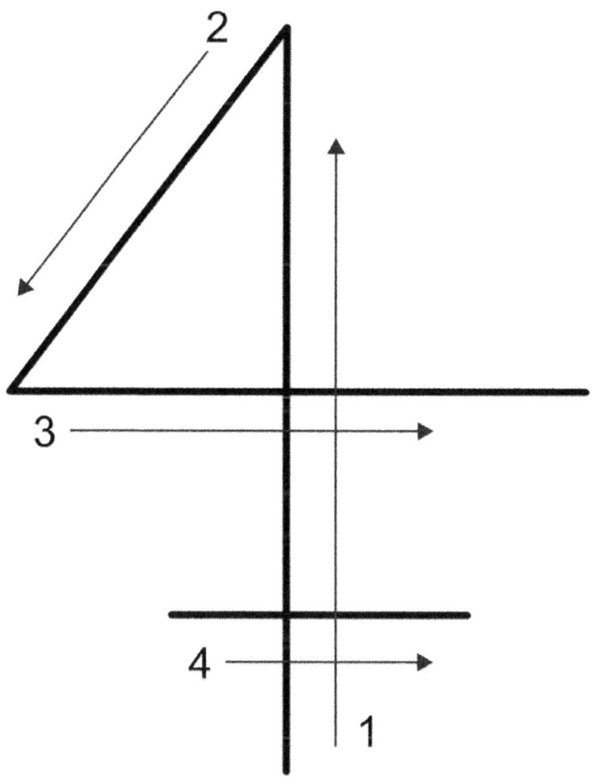

Perfect Love And Trust was channeled by Reiki Master Jamie Gallant and aligns with the universal concepts of self-respect, love, compassion, acceptance, and trust. It doesn't belong to any specific Reiki system but carries a powerful vibration that can benefit spiritual and personal growth.

Attributes:

- **Self-Respect:** Encourages recognizing and valuing oneself, treating oneself with dignity and care;
- **Love:** Promotes a profound sense of love for oneself and others, encompassing compassion and empathy;
- **Compassion:** Extends love and empathy to all living beings, recognizing the interconnectedness of life;
- **Acceptance:** Helps in accepting oneself and others, fostering understanding and patience;
- **Trust:** Aids in building trust in oneself and others, a foundational aspect of healthy relationships;

Perfect Love and Trust has the following uses:

- Visualizing or focusing on this symbol during meditation can help you connect with its energy, allowing its principles to resonate within your being;
- Printing and displaying the symbol in your environment will help to remind you of its attributes, infusing its energy into your surroundings;
- Applying the teachings of this symbol in daily mindfulness practice can further cultivate the qualities of self-respect, love, compassion, acceptance, and trust in your life;

The Perfect Love And Trust symbol is a unique and profound tool that can guide individuals on a journey of self-awareness and spiritual awakening. Its principles align with universal values and can be a catalyst for positive transformation and a more balanced existence.

SYMBOL FOR BURNS

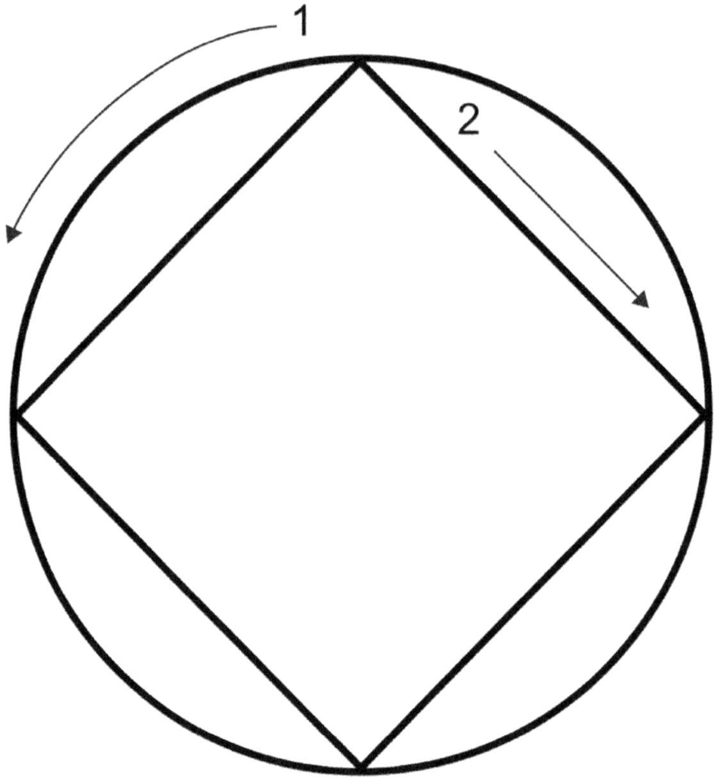

The "Symbol for Burns" is a unique and potent energetic tool that doesn't belong to any Reiki system. It is a testament to energy healing practices' versatility and adaptability.

Symbol for Burns has the following attributes:

- The symbol's essence is specifically attuned to provide soothing comfort to burned areas of the body. It acts as a gentle, energetic balm, engaging with the natural healing energies within the body to alleviate pain and expedite recovery;

Symbol for Burns has the following uses:

- Start by visualizing or drawing the Cho Ku Rei + Sei He Ki + Zonar + Symbol for Burns sequence over the affected body area. These additional symbols enhance the healing vibration, forming a powerful triad with the Symbol for Burns;

- Gently hover your hands above the targeted region, allowing the energy to flow for about 10 minutes daily. Feel the warmth of the universal energy as it works in concert with your body's innate healing ability, infusing the area with calming vibrations;

- With time and repetition, this practice supports the healing process, nourishing the skin and underlying tissues;

ANTI-POISONING

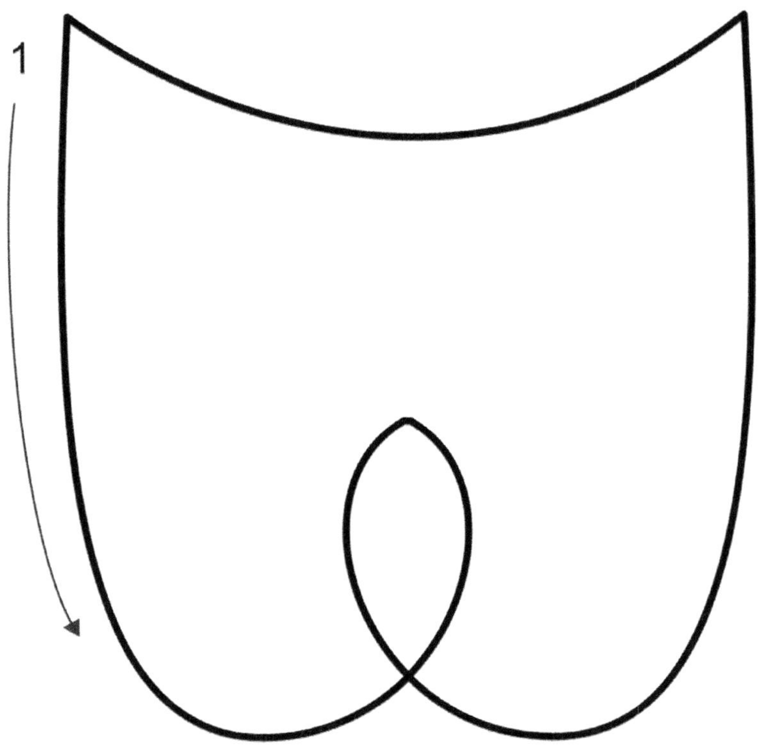

The primary focus of the Anti-Poisoning symbol is the purification and elimination of negative energies associated with various forms of poisoning. Its unique ability can help you target the root cause through a non-invasive approach that can support traditional methods in restoring physical vitality.

Anti-Poisoning has the following attribute:

- The ability to identify and dissolve the residual and negative energies linked to the bacteria, viruses, or other agents responsible for poisoning. It targets the core of the problem, working at an energetic level to cleanse and restore balance;

Anti-Poisoning has the following uses:

- Connect with the symbol by visualizing or activating it physically on your crown chakra. You may feel a sensation as it begins to resonate with your energy field;

- Slowly guide the symbol's energy through your body. Allow its purifying essence to flow freely, seeking out the toxins and pathogens. Imagine it as a gentle yet powerful stream, washing away the poison and restoring harmony to the affected areas;

NOTE: *Remember that the effectiveness of poison removal with this symbol is intricately connected to your overall energy vibration level. Your belief, intention, and openness to the process will amplify its efficacy.*

DRAGONFLY

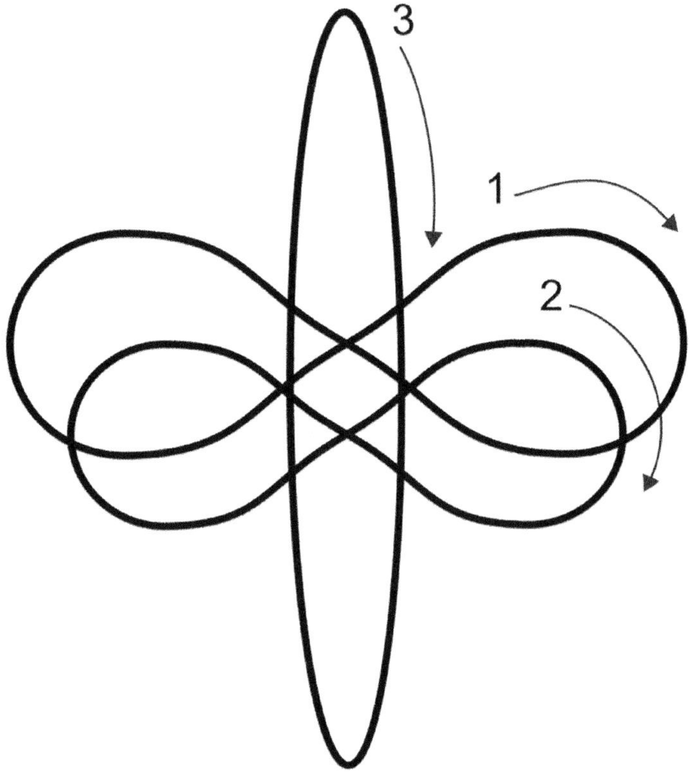

The Dragonfly symbol is a unique emblem that transcends any particular Reiki system. It was channeled by the esteemed Reiki Master Jessica Arsenault and serves as an extraordinary tool to awaken clarity, harmony, and compassion within oneself and in interactions with others.

Dragonfly Symbol has the following attributes:

- The Dragonfly symbol has the powerful ability to shatter life-related illusions that may be imposed by others or even self-inflicted. It offers a clear and unobstructed view of reality, helping to free the mind from misconceptions and deceptive thoughts;

- If tension and discord dominate your workspace, the Dragonfly symbol can be invoked to create a harmonious atmosphere. It radiates an energy that fosters collaboration, understanding, and balance among colleagues;

- This symbol transcends mere surface-level connections, igniting compassion, empathy, and genuine understanding between people. It helps dissolve barriers and creates a bridge to deeper connections;

Dragonfly Symbol has the following uses:

- Activate it on your crown and throat chakras before engaging with a group of people. This activation process helps you break free from preconceived notions or past patterns. It clears the way for fresh perspectives, enabling you to approach situations without biases or judgments;

- By invoking the Dragonfly symbol, you cultivate an environment where unconditional love and compassion flourish. It creates a space for honest dialogue, genuine care, and mutual respect;

The Dragonfly symbol is a dynamic energy that surfaces your ability to clarify, harmonize, and foster healthy interactions. By integrating the Dragonfly symbol into your daily practices, you embrace a journey of authenticity, empathy, and collaboration, allowing you to navigate life's complexities with grace and wisdom.

ANESTHESIA

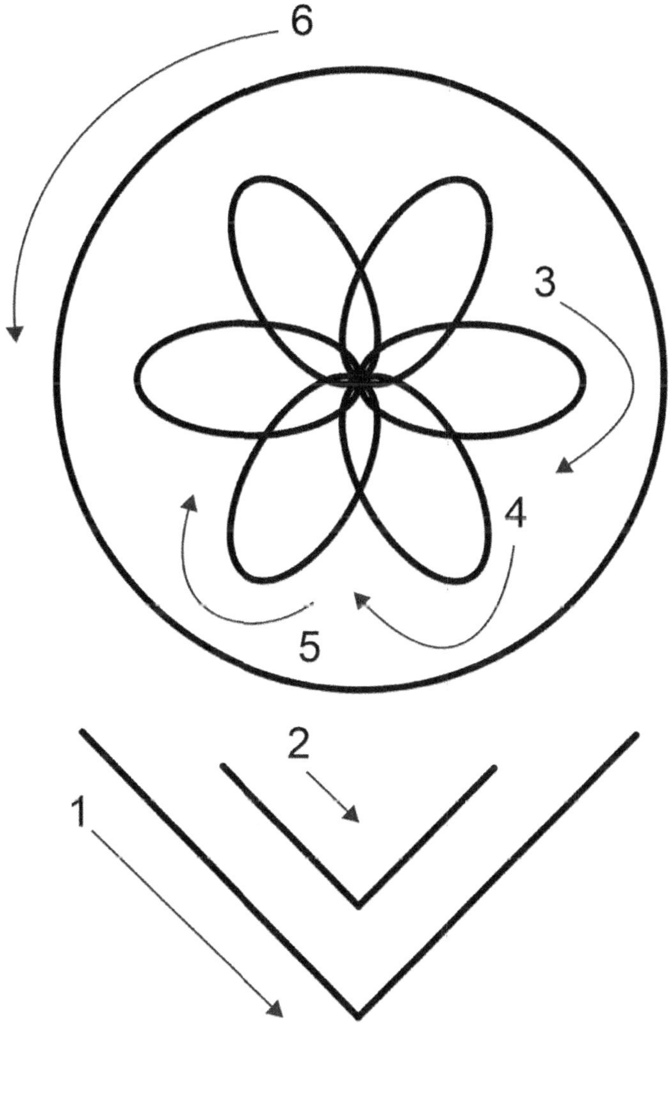

The Anesthesia symbol was channeled by renowned Reiki Master Susan Isabel and doesn't belong to any particular Reiki system. It serves as a spiritual tool that can bring temporary relief from physical discomfort.

Anesthesia has the following attributes:

- As the name suggests, the Anesthesia symbol's primary function is to temporarily numb specific areas of the body. Whether you're grappling with acute pain or seeking to reduce sensation during a procedure, this symbol offers a non-invasive means of easing discomfort;

- Beyond mere numbing, the Anesthesia symbol is infused with an energy that can soothe and calm inflamed or wounded body parts. Its gentle vibrations promote healing, providing a nurturing environment for the body's natural recuperation;

Anesthesia has the following uses:

- To harness the healing power of the Anesthesia symbol, one must visualize or draw it over the affected area as a three-dimensional structure. This process requires focused intention and an openness to receiving the symbol's energy;

- It works with pinpoint precision, allowing you to target specific regions that require attention. Its energy is adaptable, making it suitable for various physical concerns;

The Anesthesia symbol can provide tangible relief from physical ailments while resonating with the soul's innate healing abilities. It's not just a metaphorical anesthesia but an actual energetic tool that you can apply to real situations.

JOINT HEALING

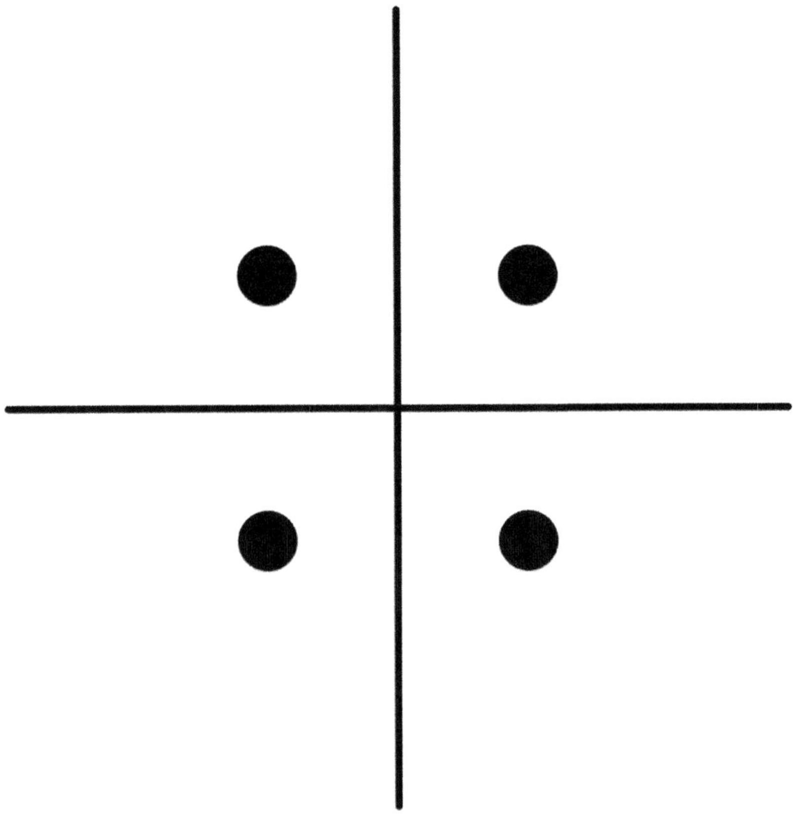

The Joint Healing symbol belongs to the Violet Flame Reiki system. It holds a unique place for its targeted healing energy, focusing on the complex and often delicate areas of muscles and joints.

Joint Healing has the following attributes:

- Healing muscle and joint sprains;
- Repairing dislocations;
- Mending meniscus ruptures;
- Relieving joint and muscle pains;

Joint Healing has the following uses:

- To utilize the healing properties of the Joint Healing symbol, one must activate it directly on the affected area;
- Add Cho Ku Rei to enhance the healing effect, enveloping the area in a nurturing, restorative embrace;

The Joint Healing symbol works in harmony with the body's intrinsic healing abilities, offering support where it's needed most.

The Journey Continues

We've covered a lot of ground and so many fascinating symbols. This section is a reminder that we're not aiming to reach a final destination but to find the bridge toward continuous exploration.

You've now gained a profound understanding of these powerful symbols, and with this knowledge in hand, the real journey of personal and spiritual growth truly begins.

This last part includes various tools, ideas, and concepts to help you foster a deeper and more harmonious connection with Reiki symbols.

Blessings

Blessings are a heartfelt gesture you can extend in specific situations. They weave their magic in every religion and spiritual practice as highly influential acts of love. At their core lies a surge of positive energy that can bolster a person, action, or event, guiding it toward the greater good.

I encourage you to bless the actions and words of anyone who might have wronged you. Do it in the name of the Divine, making it your mission to transform those negative vibrations into positive ones.

In essence, what you're doing is akin to alchemy. With each blessing, you're turning lead into gold and darkness into light, inviting more positivity into your life and, by extension, into the world. Each blessing is a tiny pebble creating ripples of love and understanding in the vast ocean of life.

Symbols In Practice

Let's explore the infinite potential of Reiki symbols through some real-life examples.

When I was first learning Reiki, my teacher would divide his seminars into two distinct parts:

- The first hour was dedicated to treating patients, which allowed us to learn about Reiki therapy and other spiritual practices;
- The second hour, which would naturally emerge from the first, focused on discussing various topics, with plenty of opportunities to ask questions;

This process gradually fed our curiosity and helped us understand the concepts discussed that day. We didn't just gain technical know-how but also became more attuned to the spiritual aspects of healing, appreciating the interconnectedness of mind, body, and spirit.

We learned about Reiki symbols in many ways. Still, probably the most significant memories stick due to the examples we had the privilege to go through. Let's discuss a few of them that hopefully shed new light on applying Reiki symbols beyond their meaning and scope.

Neutralizing The Quicksilver Intruder

One of my earliest experiences with Reiki symbols goes back to when my first Reiki teacher handled a relatively common case.

A middle-aged woman came to our office, disturbed by her constant abdominal pain, frequent nausea, and dizziness that had been persisting for a while. Despite medical examinations, nothing abnormal was found. At this point, my Reiki teacher did what he excelled at: he began asking the pertinent questions.

Early on, I learned that a critical element in applying an efficient treatment is understanding what you need to address before deciding how to approach a situation. This can only result from asking the right questions and embracing the truth instead of avoiding the reality that got you there. Of course, it takes experience, but it's one skill we should all aspire to improve.

It didn't take long before she mentioned an argument with a relative who also happened to practice dark arts. Going back through the chain of events, she realized that her abdominal discomfort had started soon after. My teacher recognized this as a "quicksilver" issue, which could be either intentionally projected onto her or absorbed. Without hesitation, he applied Cho Ku Rei + Sei He Ki + Zonar + Halu to her primary chakras, intending to dissolve and remove the quicksilver energy. We all supported his efforts by channeling universal energy to the patient. Surprisingly, in less than 10 minutes, her state significantly improved. The pain "miraculously" vanished when she got home, and, in just a few days, her digestive system resumed its normal routine.

With a clear intention developed through a quick but thorough analysis of the problem, accompanied by a specific sequence of Reiki symbols, my teacher was able to dissolve the negative energies related to the issue, creating room for the pure light to enter and heal the body.

Stabilizing Chaotic Energy Flows

The second example involves another woman who visited my teacher's practice after a pilgrimage to Saint Andrew's cave, a location revered for its sacred, high-vibrational energy in Romania. Notably, she was particularly sensitive to energetic changes.

Following her trip, she experienced persistent pain in her sacral area and a distinct tingling sensation along her spine. Furthermore, during Reiki treatments, her body began to make uncontrollable, snake-like movements that resembled waves of energy pulsating through her.

From an energetic perspective, it appeared that her Kundalini energy had awakened suddenly but without proper management, causing a chaotic energy flow that manifested as abrupt physical movements.

Recognizing the need for a different approach, I activated two potent Reiki symbols: The Serpent of Fire on her backside and the Dragon of Fire on her front. The goal was to soothe and temporarily ground her Kundalini energy, facilitating a more gradual and harmonious awakening. Remarkably, her erratic movements subsided within minutes, allowing us to proceed with a more comprehensive treatment.

Subsequent Reiki sessions were needed for her Kundalini energy to fully stabilize and for her sensitivity to energy fluctuations to become manageable.

Transforming Desolation Into Vitality

This third example comes from when I attended another mentor's seminar.

One day, a businesswoman who had been a long-time student of his rushed into his practice before a flight she was scheduled to catch that afternoon. Recently, she had gone through a breakup and was overwhelmed with a variety of emotions. Unable to achieve a balanced emotional state on her own, she sought additional help.

My teacher took a straightforward approach, projecting a Sei He Ki symbol over her entire physical body. He declared a clear intention to neutralize the negative energies fueling her feelings of sadness and anxiety. Within a few minutes, the patient began to feel more relaxed and breathed with greater confidence. He then activated Usui and Karuna Reiki symbols on her primary chakras, providing rapid treatment.

The exciting part of the lesson was that my teacher absorbed a significant portion of that energy. He began to feel sad, hopeless, and anxious as the low-vibrational energies manifested within his own energy fields. However, he anticipated this and immediately started a self-cleansing process.

In conclusion, the entire procedure proved successful, and the patient resumed her daily activities with renewed optimism and vitality. She made her flight, and her meeting yielded a favorable result.

It's important to note that the Reiki symbols didn't achieve this on their own. My teacher's clear intention and vast experience were instrumental in guiding everything toward the best possible outcome.

A Reiki Project That Won My Heart

Days before my final exams as a senior in high school, anxiety took over my life, and gloomy scenarios dominated my thoughts. I didn't know much about Reiki back then, but looking back, I'm amazed at how simple procedures helped me, even though I was only equipped with a fraction of what I know today.

At the time, I decided to use the Cho Ku Rei + Sei He Ki + Hon Sha Ze Sho Nen sequence of Reiki symbols to empower a Reiki project, adding a unique twist. Feeling that I had nothing to lose, I pursued this idea. I drew a triangle with large circles adjacent to each corner on a piece of paper. At the top, I wrote my goal, clearly stating my desire to pass the exam with the highest grade possible. On the right corner, I added "Divine Intervention." I included the Reiki symbols combination I mentioned earlier in the left corner.

In the days leading up to the exam, I began sending universal energy to this project for my greater good. To my amazement, on the test day, I "randomly" chose the subject I was best prepared for and aced it! It felt like a perfect dream, almost too good to be true. That was one of the moments that stayed with me, making the possibilities of Reiki come alive in my heart.

Takeaway

While the examples I've given might seem impressive at first glance, they demonstrate the practicality of Reiki symbols in balancing energy structures and dispelling negative energies. However, if you pay close attention, a common thread runs through all these examples - each approach was paired with a clear intention and the actual transfer of universal life force energy.

It's crucial to remember that the connection, flow, and manifestation of universal life force energy underpin the practice, with the symbols acting as facilitators for specific manifestations required at each moment. This makes the symbols very useful but not indispensable. To reinforce this idea, let me share my experience from the 100th-year celebration of Reiki, held in Osaka, Japan:

At the start and end of each event day, the Japanese masters Hiroshi Doi and Hyakuten Inamoto guided us through a meditation intended to refresh our connection to the universal life force energy. Not once did they mention the use of Reiki symbols. Instead, they emphasized the unshakeable value of our connection to the source of universal life force energy. True mastery lies in being perfectly in tune with the source of universal life force energy, capable of manifesting its different frequencies whenever needed, without the reliance on symbols. You are the spirit that will always be one with this energy!

Remember, the symbols are the jewels of Reiki, but they are not the practice itself!

When Symbols Whisper

Have you ever felt an inexplicable connection to a symbol? Well... You're not alone! Many individuals resonate with specific signs within the vast world of spirituality.

Imagine you're drifting off to sleep or meditating, and a symbol keeps appearing in your visions or dreams. It might challenge you to overcome a hurdle or push you to aim for a higher level. It's not merely a reflection of your spiritual awareness but a guide toward growth.

The meaning of these symbols isn't one-size-fits-all. Each person's unique spiritual path and life choices will lead to a vast array of interpretations.

Remember, each symbol can manifest universal energy, which could be as gentle as a summer breeze or as powerful as a roaring storm. Also, entities support this energy's existence, and through each symbol, you can tap into this information.

The symbols that appear in your visions, dreams, or meditations can fall into three categories:

- Symbols not linked to any specific system or practice;
- Symbols from outside the Reiki systems;
- Symbols from a Reiki system, whether you are attuned to it or not;

So, what should you do if you find a symbol knocking at the door? If there's a beneficial connection between you and that symbol, start by drawing its shape and begin nurturing your relationship.

It's also likely that you won't find much about it online or in books. This shouldn't stop you! If you sense its genuine value, use the integration meditation provided in this guide to further tap into its energetic print.

Next, use it in your Reiki self-treatment and be alert to any shifts within your healing process. Notice the subtle changes that might be happening. If the outcomes are pleasing, you can confidently embrace the symbol as an extension of your energy fields. Celebrate this special bond and be thankful for the gift you just received!

Here's what to do if things don't go as planned:

- Continue with your practices and meditations, leaving everything as it is;

- Use the integration meditation process in reverse. Picture the energy and information of the symbol slowly detaching from your fields and entire body. Seal the process with a Cho Ku Rei;

When you find yourself visualizing a symbol or a series of symbols repeatedly, it's not by chance. There's a reason behind this pattern. They are calling for your attention, asking for your understanding and willingness to make use of their potential in serving yourself as well as others. So, take on this challenge and embrace the opportunity to delve deeper to unravel their mysteries. Be happy and grateful for this opportunity, and always trust that you're on the right path, even if it may not look as expected.

The symbol that shows up repeatedly in your dreams or meditations can be one of your choosing, a sign you have a personal connection with. It might hold special significance for you, and understanding its purpose can be enlightening, providing valuable insights into your spiritual journey. It could positively impact your life in ways you've never imagined. The relationship you develop with these spiritual tokens can lead to an enriching and transformative experience. Your journey to uncovering the true potential of these symbols is just commencing.

Keep going!

21 Pragmatic Answers To Your Burning Questions

1) Do I need multiple attunements to use the symbols presented in this guide?

Being attuned to either level 1 or 2 in Usui Reiki means you possess enhanced access to the universal life force energy. This, in turn, provides a foundation for spiritual growth, lifting your vibration with each attunement.

This elevated access to the universal life force energy allows you to tap into any symbol you resonate with, assuming your vibration aligns with it. While this process might take more time than receiving a formal attunement, patience and discipline will enable you to integrate, at least partially, the energy print of that specific symbol.

Suppose you are attuned at least to the Usui Reiki level 2. In that case, you can utilize the meditation for integration outlined in this guide. It's designed to stimulate your ability to harness the energy and information of any symbol featured in this manual. Hence, while multiple attunements can enhance your experience, they are not strictly necessary to use the symbols presented in this guide.

2) Are these symbols harmful, or can they lead to side effects?

The symbols presented in this guide are high-vibrational representations designed to bring forth positive aspects of the universal life force energy. Their primary function is to purify, heal, or mitigate various imbalances. Yet, as with any potent tool, discretion and ethical considerations should always be top of mind. So, take responsibility for applying these symbols when working with others.

3) Aren't Reiki symbols sacred, and shouldn't they be kept secret?

Sacred? - Yes. Secret? - No. The secrecy surrounding Reiki symbols was historically rooted in a time when spiritual practices were often misunderstood, criticized, and marginalized, leading them to be concealed from the wider public. The sacredness of these symbols, however, isn't derived from their secrecy but from their intrinsic value.

The gradual dissemination of Reiki teachings and symbols in the US and Europe post-1970s demonstrates this shift in understanding. Today, these symbols are as openly available in many resources as various other religious and sacred symbols.

4) Does this guide include all symbols that can be used in a Reiki practice?

This guide certainly does not encompass all the symbols that could potentially be utilized in a Reiki practice. The Reiki world is vast, with a multitude of symbols available for exploration. The ones included in this guide are those that I have personally studied, encountered, or used in my own practice. It's my belief that by sharing these symbols, others may also reap the benefits of their healing potential.

5) What is the difference between "The Ultimate Reiki Symbols Guide" and a regular book on Reiki?

Unlike a conventional Reiki book that you might read once and then tuck away on a shelf, "The Ultimate Reiki Symbols Guide" is crafted to be an ongoing resource. It's less of a read-once book and more of a constantly referenced handbook.

The guide offers not only the spiritual significance of the symbols but also their practical applications. It's designed to be your reliable companion when other sources are out of reach or fail to provide comprehensive information. It serves as an ongoing support in your Reiki journey rather than a static piece of literature.

6) Is this the last version of "The Ultimate Reiki Symbols Guide" ever made?

Certainly not. As we continue to expand our understanding and wisdom, our products, including "The Ultimate Reiki Symbols Guide," will also evolve. The realm of Reiki is dynamic and expansive, and as we journey further into it, there will always be more to discover, learn, and share. So, you can anticipate future versions of this guide as our exploration progresses.

7) How can I deepen my connection with a specific Reiki symbol?

Strengthening your bond with a specific Reiki symbol largely comes down to regular practice and dedicated intention. The "Integration Meditation" outlined in this guide is designed to assist you in assimilating the energy and insights of the symbol, but the continuity of practice truly anchors this harmonious connection. The deeper your engagement, the stronger and more profound your connection with the symbol will become.

8) I can't seem to connect with a particular Reiki symbol. What should I do?

If you're finding it difficult to resonate with a specific Reiki symbol, don't pressure yourself into forging a connection. Instead, take a moment to step back and introspect. Perhaps inner resistance or unresolved emotions need your attention first. Approach this from a place of self-understanding, and in due time, the integration with the symbol will naturally occur. Remember, every journey of growth has its own unique pace.

9) How long does it take to fully integrate a Reiki symbol into my practice?

The timeline for fully integrating a Reiki symbol into your practice can vary greatly and is deeply personal. It depends on factors such as resolving mental and emotional blockages, your current vibration, and understanding levels. Some symbols carry a high vibration that might not initially align with your current state, requiring a period of adjustment. The key is patience and openness to this transformative process.

10) How long do the effects of using a Reiki symbol last?

The effects of using a Reiki symbol can last anywhere from a few minutes to several hours, depending on the quality of your connection to the universal life force energy and your current vibrational level.

It's a deeply individual experience and can vary from person to person and session to session. Remember, the potency of the symbols stems from your intention and focus, not just the duration of their effects.

11) What should I do if a Reiki symbol makes me feel uncomfortable?

If a Reiki symbol makes you feel uncomfortable, it's often a sign that there may be unresolved emotional or mental imbalances that are affecting your connection to universal energy.

The symbol's vibrations could stir these imbalances, leading to feelings of discomfort, a sense of being overwhelmed, or even physical sensations like a burning feeling. Regular use of the Reiki self-treatment in conjunction with these symbols can help you navigate and resolve these issues, leading to a more harmonious and beneficial connection with the symbols.

12) What does it mean if a Reiki symbol appears to me in a dream?

If a Reiki symbol appears in your dream, it could suggest that you share a unique and special bond with that symbol. This is particularly true if it's a symbol you haven't seen before. Such occurrences invite further exploration and attunement with the symbol, potentially revealing new layers of understanding and connection in your Reiki practice.

13) Do I need to use the symbols every time I do a Reiki session?

While the Reiki symbols are powerful tools to help channel and amplify the universal life force energy, their use in every Reiki session is not mandatory. Your Reiki practice extends beyond just using symbols. It's ultimately about your intuitive connection to the energy and how you choose to facilitate its flow and healing potential.

14) Can the use of Reiki symbols replace the self-treatment process?

No, Reiki symbols should not be viewed as a replacement for self-treatment. Instead, they are meant to enhance and complement your self-treatment process. The symbols help remove negative energy and ensure a smoother flow of pure energy.

You may also use them to nourish spiritual growth by allowing you to tap into various facets of the universal life force energy. Yet, the practice of self-treatment remains a crucial component.

15) Is there a risk of overusing or misusing a Reiki symbol?

Reiki energy, by its nature, is safe and benign. However, using Reiki symbols with ill intent can result in imbalances or unintended consequences. It's important to adhere to ethical guidelines when using Reiki symbols and to always approach your Reiki practice and others with respect and positive intentions.

16) Do I need to be re-attuned if I've forgotten a Reiki symbol?

No, there's no need for re-attunement if you've forgotten a Reiki symbol. The meditation for integration outlined in this guide, combined with regular practice, will aid in re-establishing your connection with the energy and wisdom encapsulated by that particular symbol.

17) Can I use Reiki symbols in my daily life outside of a healing session?

Absolutely! In fact, one of the main goals of this manual is to demonstrate the versatile use of Reiki symbols, extending beyond just healing sessions.

18) Can I create my own Reiki symbol?

It's not so much that you're creating a new Reiki symbol but channeling an existing energetic imprint from the divine consciousness. This imprint is designed to assist us in our earthly experiences. It's about tuning into something already conceived in the realm of divine energy.

19) If I use the meditation for integrating symbols', does this mean I also attune myself to the corresponding system?

No. This meditation doesn't equate to self-attunement in the corresponding Reiki system. It is designed to facilitate your use of the symbols outside the context of an attunement. Still, it doesn't eliminate the necessity for a formal attunement from a Reiki Master to fully unlock the potential of that symbol.

20) Does "The Ultimate Reiki Symbols Guide" contain any attunements?

No. Aside from the meditations, which act as tools for helping you become in tune with the energy of the presented symbols, there are no actual attunements given through "The Ultimate Reiki Symbols Guide."

21) Can I teach the Reiki symbols to others? If so, how?

Sharing knowledge about Reiki symbols is a beautiful way to promote holistic healing and spiritual growth. If you're familiar with a symbol, you can share its meaning and applications and guide others through meditation.

However, as a certified Reiki Master-Teacher, you're qualified to offer formal attunements, unlocking the full potential of Reiki symbols corresponding to a specific Reiki system. Always teach responsibly and ethically.

Ethical Considerations

Being mindful of certain aspects when channeling universal energy is crucial for a beneficial and pleasant experience for both the practitioner and the receiver.

When you practice Reiki on yourself, it's important to be aware that you'll also influence the people around you by the heightened vibration you cultivate. They may feel the effects of this energetic shift, both internally and in the surrounding space. Over time, they will gradually adapt to this new vibration. However, in the initial stages, they may feel a sense of not fully belonging to that space anymore.

If you choose to use Reiki methods or symbols in a public setting, it's essential to be aware that you are also cleansing and altering the existing vibrations.

In addition, not everyone may understand or agree with what you are doing. Therefore, unless specifically requested, it is best to find a quiet place to practice and utilize your Reiki techniques.

When Practicing Reiki On Others, Consent Matters

When offering Reiki to others, obtaining their consent is of utmost importance. There are two situations you want to be aware of:

- When an individual asks for personal Reiki assistance, whether in a physical setting or through distance healing;
- When an individual seeks help regarding specific issues, such as relationships or life goals. In this case, always use your Reiki knowledge to aid that particular concept and not the people involved;

To better support an ethical approach and promote an optimum flow rather than doing things randomly, always channel the universal energy:

"For the greater good of the relationship and the people involved, aligned with the divine laws."

NOTE: *As a Reiki practitioner who has been attuned to the practice, it is your responsibility to offer Reiki in an optimal, beneficial, and guided manner when helping or teaching others. You are accountable for their well-being during those moments and should provide the necessary guidelines for them to practice mindfully. Once you do that, knowing that each individual is responsible for their actions moving forward is also essential.*

Final Thoughts

We've embarked on an incredible journey together, haven't we? I hope that the wisdom in "The Ultimate Reiki Symbols Guide" has enlightened your path and will continue to serve as your companion on this spiritual voyage. Now, I'd like to leave you with a few key takeaways.

First, embrace the joy of 'bite-size learning.' This isn't just about avoiding the sensation of being overwhelmed but about savoring each piece of wisdom, letting it seep into your being, and cultivating a more profound understanding before moving on to the following enlightening detail.

Never forget you are the master conductor of the universal life force energy, orchestrating the flow of positivity and wellness into your life. Each element you resonate with is not just a symbol but a new friend. Forge deep, meaningful relationships with these symbols, nurturing your spiritual side and fostering your personal growth.

Imagine the waves of positivity emanating from you as you shift your energy and habits, impacting not just your life but the world around you. Gradually, you are becoming the architect of your own destiny, building it brick by brick with the universal life force energy.

Remember: this guide is the beginning of your transformative journey with Reiki symbols. Thank you for joining me on this enlightening journey!

Keep shining, keep growing, and continue spreading your light into the world.

Bibliography:

Argesanu, Ovidiu-Dragos. *Reiki Intre Mit Si Realitate (Romanian Edition).* ProDao, 2014.

Argesanu, Ovidiu-Dragos. *The PSY Attack: Between Science and Magic.* ProDao, 2022.

Argesanu, Ovidiu-Dragos. *The Art of Psy War - Protection.* ProDao, 2015.

Penczak, Christopher. *Magick Of Reiki - Focused on Energy For Healing, Ritual & Spiritual Development.* Llewellyn Publications, 2004.

Risvan, Vlad-Rusu. *Dictionar De Simboluri Pentru Protectia Spirituala (Romanian Edition).* Editura Trinity, 2015.

Risvan, Vlad-Rusu. *Karuna - Vindecare Naturala Cu Ingeri Arhangheli si Lumina (Romanian Edition).* Editura Trinity, 2012.

Albu, Mihai. *Reiki – O Metoda Practica.* Lifestyle Publishing, 2014.

Printed in Great Britain
by Amazon

50106697R00142